THAI VALUES AND
BEHAVIOR PATTERNS

THAI VALUES AND BEHAVIOR PATTERNS

by Robert L. Mole

CHARLES E. TUTTLE COMPANY
Rutland, Vermont & Tokyo, Japan

Representatives

Continental Europe: BOXERBOOKS, INC., *Zurich*

British Isles: PRENTICE-HALL INTERNATIONAL, INC., *London*

Australasia: PAUL FLESCH & CO., PTY. LTD., *Melbourne*

Canada: M. G. HURTIG LTD., *Edmonton*

Published by the Charles E. Tuttle Company, Inc.
of Rutland, Vermont & Tokyo, Japan
with editorial offices at
Suido 1-chome, 2-6, Bunkyo-ku, Tokyo, Japan

Copyright in Japan, 1973 by Charles E. Tuttle Co., Inc.

Library of Congress Catalog Card No. 71-130419

International Standard Book No. 0-8048-0947-x

First edition, 1973

PRINTED IN JAPAN

TABLE OF CONTENTS

FOREWORD

It is always ideal to know as much as possible about those one works with and among. This is especially true in cross-cultural situations. To understand and appreciate potential courses of advice or action, it is wise to know the personalities and backgrounds of those with whom encounters are frequent. Non-indigenous peoples can best establish friendly relationships through knowledge of language, customs, foods, history, social conditions, etc. When these avenues of rapport are utilized, cross-cultural ideas are more readily transferrable and acceptable due to greater validity of understanding of aspirations, problems and steps of "progress".

Through identification and awareness of the roles performed by the various cultural elements, the "outsider" has a greater sense of ease. This, combined with knowledge, permits a more effective performance whatever may be the assignment. It is essential, however, to always identify the Thai as an individual within his culture even as the American desires recognition and acceptance as a unique person, and not just a number within the approximately two hundred million of America. The complexities of an alien, or different, culture may be perplexing at first, but can be solved if one cares enough to really try.

To provide assistance in developing a knowledge of indigenous

religions, customs, traditions and people, the United States Navy
and the United States Marines have instituted a transcultural endeavor
known as Personal Response. Navy or Marine Personal Response is
a systematic effort in intercultural attitude changes predicated upon
awareness, understanding and appreciation of cultural-belief-value-
systems which determine behavior patterns.

This cross-cultural endeavor is currently sponsored and
supported by Rear Admiral James W. KELLY, CHC, USN, Chief
of Chaplain, United States Navy; the Commandant, United States
Marines: and by Rear Admiral Walter COMBS, Jr., Commander
Service Force, U.S. Pacific Fleet. This new dimension of the
Navy/Marine Team in Southeast Asia seems to remedy the deficiencies
of transcultural understanding between Americans and their allies.
Awareness, appreciation and consideration of value-belief-behavioral
patterns can be of significant value in the achievement of objectives
assigned to Navy/Marine personnel.

THAI VALUES AND PRACTICES is a technical study prepared
for submission to the Director of the Center for South and Southeast
Studies, American University, Dr. Kenneth P. LANDON. The study
was performed under Navy sponsorship in support of Navy Personal
Response. The title of the original study was A CRITICAL EVALUATION

OF THE INTER-RELATIONSHIPS BETWEEN THE VALUE SYSTEMS
AND PRACTICES OF THE PEOPLE OF THAILAND.

While attempting to meet university academic specifications, the imperative "need to know" requirements have strongly influenced the information included in this study. Although limited in scope and volume, this edition contains sufficient information to serve as a launching-pad for explorations through cultural barriers for a better tomorrow. This is an experimental edition prepared and produced under combat conditions in South Vietnam. Critical comments, suggestions or additional information that will enhance the validity of this and similar studies will be deeply appreciated.

ROBERT L. MOLE

The Marble Temple in Bangkok illustrates the architectural beauty ▶
and splendor of many Thai buildings. It houses a museum of ancient
images of Buddha and was built in 1910.

His Royal Majesty King
Bhumibol Adulyadej of
Thailand is shown while
serving as a Buddhist monk.
The king, who was born in
Cambridge, Mass., where his
father was a student at
Harvard University Medical
school, is well known as
a jazz musician and composer
and is a symbol of Thai unity.

Women of the Meo tribe watch with interest one of the children of
the tribe who was adopted by an American missionary dentist after
the child's mother died and the father was unable to take care of him.

◀ These two large statues of Buddha demonstrate the powerful
Buddhist religious influences in Thailand. Above is reclining
Buddha statue which is located outside Bangkok. It symbolizes the
passing of Buddha into Nibbana. Below is a modern Buddha statue
found in Bangkok.

The center for tribal studies
on the campus of the University of Chieng Mai is shown
here. If the knowledge acquired and shared here is
effectively implemented, a
new understanding of ethnic
relations will be a reality.

Hard work begins early for
girls from a Meo village.
These girls at four years of
age carry water from a stream
flowing near their village.

The elephant is an important economic asset in Thai forests. A "White" elephant is a symbol of good fortune since Buddha is thought to have been a white elephant in a previous existence.

Rivers in Thailand are a means of transportation, a source of food, and vital for irrigation and domestic usage. This village is on the River Kwai. Many of the houses are on bamboo floats so that the rainy seasons pose no serious problems.

A chedi found within ancient ruins reveals some of the impact made by the Indian cultural influences in Thailand.

CHAPTER ONE

WHY THAILAND ?

Twentieth century realities include awareness that the United States is the major political-economic-military force thwarting the expansion of communism. This unique position requires that the United States make and implement major policy decisions throughout the world. The Asia-Pacific region shares with the Europe-Atlantic community the essential problems of socio-economic development or decay, peace and prosperity or internal and international conflicts.

The Asia-Pacific community contains more than half of the world's population. Thus important developments in the Pacific Basin have significant effects upon the socio-economic-military health of the world. Within the larger Pacific community is that of Southeast Asia with its two hundred fifty million people divided into ten nations. While constituting only a small part of the Asian population, Southeast Asia's geographic location may give it the key to the future of Asia. The past few years have allowed most of its countries to display significant economic gains while developing pragmatic political leaders, building political institutions and establishing deeper commitments of regional cooperation.

The fateful decision of the United States to maintain its presence in this region is of crucial importance to the Southeast Asians and to the Americans. There are but few current political leaders in Southeast Asia who do not recognize how much different the political fate of the whole region would be without this economic-political-military presence. Moreover, development and stability of the whole area is of vital importance to America, for besides being the foremost world power at the present, the United States is a Pacific as well as an Atlantic nation.

Thailand is the largest of the Southeast Asian nations located on the Asian mainland. Moreover the Kingdom of Thailand is strategically important to the total American effort in the Pacific Basin. It's location, almost completely surrounded by newer nations which have known independence from Western rule for only a short time, provides a bulwark in an otherwise communist infested area. Additionally, Thailand's food producing capabilities gives it a position of economic importance beyond its population of about thirty million. More significantly to the United

States is the fact that Thailand's national objectives parallel those of the United States in the area. Thus, the United States assists the Royal Thai Government improve its capabilities in the development of the Kingdom economically, politically and socially behind a shield of internal security and joint military defense against insurgency.

United States interest in Thailand derives from interest in East Asia as a whole, and its perception of Thailand's role in preserving that interest. Since the last century, the United States objective has been basically to prevent any one nation dominating the area. Because the United States believes a one-nation domination of East Asia is a threat to United States security, it engaged in an economic and, eventually, military war with Japan. Since then, it has subsequently risked major war several other times. In October 1966 while in Hawaii, the President of the United States publicly and explicitly re-affirmed American national interest in the area when he said "No single nation can or should be permitted to dominate the Pacific region".

This was stated even more strongly for Thailand in June 1967 when President Lyndon B. Johnson said, "The United States ... regards the preservation of the independence and integrity of Thailand as vital to the national interests of the United States and to world peace."

Consequently, with the rise of the Communist Chinese regime, United States relations with Thailand have changed from general friendship and good will to a close alliance backed by commitments of the most serious nature. The United States regards this alliance as essential to the attainments of its own objectives in Southeast Asia. Accordingly, it has focused its concerns and provided resources for the preservation of the Thai Kingdom to a greater degree than for any other nation faced with a comparable level of insurgency.

Communist China's objectives including the preservation of national polity and security; the extension of influence in Asia; recognition as a great world power and leadership of the communist world, would be advanced by the attainment of a dominant position in Southeast Asia. Thus, it has a natural apprehension of the attitudes displayed by those Southeast Asian countries supported by Western powers with military forces and bases on their soil. Western-oriented Southeast nations like Thailand are not only obstacles to extending Chinese communist influence into the area, but are also viewed as definite threats to its security. For more than a century before the present Peking regime, peripheral nations to China were colonized by various powers who then

4

directed their influence into China. As a result China regards any strong power in Asia as a threat to its national security. It also recognizes that the United States presence in and support of these peripheral nations is the only effective deterrent to domination of Southeast Asia and the establishment of Peking oriented governments.

Thailand in particular, by virtue of its close alliance with the United States, poses a serious problem. Communist China's interest in extending its sphere of influence, from which other powers would be excluded, dictates the establishment of a friendly government in Thailand and the removal of United States military power. To Peking, insurgency appears to offer the most effective means of accomplishing these objectives.

To forestall this communist goal and promote its own objectives for the area, United States-Thai relations have evolved from general friendship to a close alliance. In 1950 economic and military assistance agreements between the two nations were signed, followed by the Southeast Asia collective Defence Treaty (SEATO) in 1954 subsequent to the establishment of two Vietnams. By 1962 the two governments interpreted the SEATO treaty as permitting bilateral action by two or more member nations without prior agreement of other signatory nations. In that same year and in 1963, United States

5

military forces were deployed temporarily to Thailand because of the deteriorating situation in Laos.

In 1964 the President of the United States authorized bilateral U.S.–Thai military planning. The Southeast Asian situation continued to deteriorate from the American viewpoint. Therefore in 1965 American military units were deployed to Thailand to reduce the flow of North Vietnamese personnel and materials to South Vietnam. In May 1967, the United States Ambassador to Thailand stated: "For the United States, the war in Southeast Asia, focusing on Vietnam at this time, is the dominant fact controlling current American policy toward Thailand. The need for Thailand as a base of operations in Vietnam and Laos is exigent and, for the duration of the conflict, is the central consideration in our relationship".[1]

Prior to this, in 1966, President Lyndon Johnson frankly acknowledged the relationship between regional cooperation and United States interest. On that occasion he said: "Our purpose

---

1. Draft of MILITARY ADVISOR HANDBOOK THAILAND, page 1. & If approved, this Handbook will be a publication of USMACT/JUSMAGT Publication.

in promoting a world regional partnership is not without self-interest, for as they grow in strength ... we can look forward to a decline in the burden that America has had to bear in this generation".[2]

For the foreseeable future, the interests and problems of Southeast Asia, including Thailand, will be the concerns of the United States also. In harmony with such concern, there are currently some fifty thousand American servicemen stationed in Thailand. These are on widely scattered bases and sites of that strategic nation. These uniformed American citizens can either effectively aid or hinder the success of national policy through their relationships with the citizens of Thailand. The permanent objectives of the American presence in Thailand can be promoted or hindered through the attitudes, behavior and general conduct of the Americans to degrees beyond the imagination of most men.

STATEMENT OF THE PROBLEM: A CRITICAL EVALUATION OF THE INTER-RELATIONSHIPS BETWEEN THE VALUE SYSTEMS AND PRACTICES OF THE PEOPLE OF THAILAND is a study of the dynamic forces which control or stimulate behavior patterns in Thailand.

---

2. Ibid

7

M. E. Opler says that themes are the dynamic forces, be they propositions or postulates, declared or applied, which normally controls behavior or stimulus activity, tacitly approved or openly promoted, within a given society. [3] If this is true, a thorough themal analysis of Thai culture will relate one theme to another, determine counter-themes, and aid in the description of the inter-relation and balancing of the various themes. This understanding can then be utilized by foreigners in Thailand in their attempts to interpret and adjust to Thai behavior patterns when these differ from those to which the visitor to Thailand is accustomed.

The belief-value-behavior patterns of most Thai differ radically from that which the Western World often takes for granted. Without awareness and appreciation of the similarilties and differences of the two cultures, many of the best motivated actions by citizens of Thailand or the West are subject to severe misunderstanding. Wise and meaningful decisions can be made only when they are based on a deep knowledge of the culture of the involved

---

3. M. E. Opler, "Themes as Dynamic Forces in Culture", American Journal of Sociology, November 1945, (51:3)

peoples. How can effective advice be given or reasonable rapport be

established without awareness of the cultural themes that establish

priorities of importance and patterns of behavior?

> The failure to understand culture differences lead to a pair
> of fallacious beliefs. On the one hand, people start with the
> correct assumption of a common humanity and jump to the false
> conclusion that the difference between Western culture and the
> various Asian cultures are superficial; that the social sciences as
> worked out for the Western societies can be applied with compar-
> atively little changes to Asian societies or that their political prob-
> lems can be discussed in terms of comparatively simple analogies
> with the West. On the other hand, people start out with the correct
> assumption that there are quite profound differences between the
> Asian and Western societies and jump to the false conclusion that
> Asian are fundamentally different in nature from peoples of
> European descent. In fact, the wide differences between the ways
> in which people behave in different societies can be explained by
> differences in their institutions, and forms of organizations and by
> the differences in their traditional systems of belief. [4]

The American - policy maker or military man of any rate or rank -

needs to be aware that the Thai are moved by the same dynamic forces

that motivate the Westerner. Human wants and needs are quite similar

throughout the world as men search for the right answers. Yet while

human needs and drives are universal, basic differences in belief-

value systems provide differing solutions to the problems which con-

---

4. Linsay of Birker in Foreword of Thomas Welty The Asians,
Their Heritage and Their Destiny, Philadelphia: J.B. Lippincott
Company, 1963, pp. 3-4

9

front all people. Thus this study is predicated upon the hypotheses:
(1) That belief-value systems create differences of customs and
behavior patterns; (2) Behavior patterns of different cultures may
differ just as radically as do their languages; (3) Basic to all human
behavior patterns are man's concepts of himself; his place in the
universe (Weltansicht); geography, economics and history; (4) That
Thai behavior is reflective of Thai values as human behavior is
not haphazard; (5) That a correct appraisal of Thai values can provide
a valid understanding and appreciation of Thai behavior by foreigners,
and (6) That awareness, understanding and appreciation of Thai
belief-value-culture factors provide an excellent basis for deepen-
ing rapport between citizens of the two cultures while promoting
increased effectiveness in joint Thai-American activities.

Kingshill thinks that seven themes dominate the Thai villager,
if Ku Daeng is a typical Thai village. These themes are utility,
profit (which includes merit), fun, individuality, communal
responsibility, playing it safe, and "Do Good, Receive Good; Do
Evil, Receive Evil".[5] Phillips seems to believe that the main

---

5. Konard Kingshill, Ku Daeng - The Red Tomb, Bangkok,
Bangkok Christian College, 1965, pp. 7-11

10

themes or personality traits are aimed at the maintenance of individuality, privacy and self regard. To him, Thai politeness is a "social cosmetic" within a framework of cosmic unpredictability with human volition only one of several indeterminate and uncontrollable factors of existence. [6] Embree thought of the Thai patterns as being a "loosely structured" system of social relations. [7] This study seeks answers to the listed propositions so that an effective valid cross-culture project can be instituted among Americans ordered to duty in Thailand and for those Thai who are in close proximity to military installations where Americans are stationed.

METHODOLOGY: This study of Thai values and behavior and their relationships is based upon a many phased approach to its complexities. Extending over a three year period, it has included academic work in the United States and two one-year tours of duty in Southeast Asia as an officer of the United States Navy with primary duty as a cultural advisor. This assignment led to the development and implementation

6. Herbert P. Phillips, Thai Peasant Personality, Berkeley and Los Angeles, University of California Press, 1966, pp. 200-208

7. John F. Embree, "Thailand - A Loosely Structured Social System" American Anthropologist, 52:181-193 (1950)

11

of Navy/Marine Personal Response, a systematic effort in intercultural attitude improvement which in Southeast Asia involves an
understanding of the indigenous religions and culture-value-
behavior systems.

In addition to the extensive and intensive use of library
facilities in the United States, other materials have been acquired
and studied in Asia. On-site research permitted the use of
observation, prepared questionnaires, in-depth interviews with
key officials of the Royal Government of Thailand, numerous conferences with various religious figures in Thailand and with the
many students of Thai culture currently involved in some phase of
transcultural activities in Thailand. This study has also led to
participation in sociological studies which will take a number of
months to translate, codify and interpret the findings and develop
a useful cross-cultural educational program for use on a mass
level.

The multiphased approach of the study of Thai values and behavior created a number of relevant questions. Since Thailand is
more than 90% Theravadist Buddhist, what are the doctrines of
Buddhism which may have definite direct and indirect influence
on values and behavior patterns? What is the role of the Sangha

12

as a molder and preserver of social values insofar as most Thai are affected? How do the Thai laity react to and reflect Buddhist teachings in both urbanized and rural areas? Are they the same or are there any non-Buddhist concepts that dominate areas of Thai behavior, and if so, what are the relationships between them and the total pattern of values and behavior? Are the values and behavior patterns on a national level? Do the various geographic and economic factors preclude national values and behavior patterns?

Chapter II, THAI BUDDHISM, is a brief review of the origin and development of Buddhism within Thailand with limited discussions of doctrines establishing values and expected patterns of behavior. Although extremely brief, this chapter with its supporting appendices, presents the organization of Buddhism, its status as the official state religion, and the teachings which seem to have the strong influences on the Thai people in theory and fact.

Chapter III, THAI STUDENT VALUES, is a discussion of the values, beliefs and practices of Thai students in the colleges and Universities of Thailand. The viewpoints of these students are significant inasmuch as they soon occupy roles of leadership in the communities of their life work. Although student concepts may not always harmonize with realities, no single group unless it be the military or Sangha has a greater potential to reshape their society.

Chapter IV, REAL BEHAVIOR, relates Thai values to behavior patterns observed in daily life. Because a total survey would require many volumes, arbitrary selections of behavior patterns are made to keep this study in manageable proportions. A serious attempt to avoid distortion of the relationships of Thai values and behavior requires the observer to be aware that simplification is potentially dangerous. Moreover, it is recognized that discussions limited to a select number of behaviorisms must not convey the impression that the whole garment has been examined. Even were this true, the fabric of a culture is much more than the individual items of which it is composed.

Chapter V. MODERNIZATION EFFECTS ON THAI VALUE-BEHAVIOR PATTERNS is the last chapter of this study. This is then followed by the Bibliography and the several appendices. Authorities on Thai culture will say that insufficient material has been included while the non-student will despair its size. Perhaps somewhere in between the two extremes a middle way has been found.

CHAPTER II

THAI BUDDHISM

The quality of humanness within man poses problems unique to the homo sapien. Unlike other animals which appear to act and react according to instinct or training, man is required to reason in order to formulate behavior patterns predicated upon belief-value systems. Human behavior is never haphazard as it is always in harmony with unconscious or even conscious value-systems. Therefore, the consciously adopted societal value systems must be both viable and comprehensive enough to direct all manifestations of internal dynamics normal to individuals within the given society. Imperative to such studies as this is an awareness that **ambivalent** drives for individuality and personal identity are countered by needs for community and community acceptance.

A comparative study of world cultures reveals the universality of religious beliefs and practices since all peoples appear to seek means by which they can relate meaningfully to their universe. Inability to establish such an identity would quickly doom both the individual and his society. When an apparently adequate world-view has been adopted, its participants tend to formulate and practice those rites, rituals and other ceremonies believed to enhance harmony between themselves and the power or powers of their world. On-site anthropological studies reveal that most societies achieve sustained effective control best when cultural authority is embedded in, and reinforced through, religious or other traditional ceremonies charged with emotional overtones.

Inherent in mankind are the needs of emotional and physical security. As General Charles De Gaulle in The Edge of the Sword noted, man is much happier with a sense of well-being and psychic mastery of one's circumstances than when faced with uncertainty, perplexities and turmoil. Therefore a companion, and perhaps even a derivative, drive is the desire for a moral and social order. Attempts to fulfill this **universally felt need** frequently results in disparate patterns of behavior due to varying belief-value systems. The relationship between value systems and behavior patterns as found within Thailand forms the core of this short volume.

Non-Buddhists normally think of Buddhism as the religion of the Buddhist. To the Buddhist adherent, however, Buddhism is the true way of existence. Therefore, a knowledge of Theravada Buddhism's doctrines is essential for a valid understanding and appreciation of the relationship between Thai values and behavior patterns seen in the daily life of Thailand.[1] The foregoing statement is true even though the influences and practices of Brahminism and animism are obvious in Thailand at the present time.

---

1. Confer Appendix D which contains a brief discussion of the Tipitaka and lists a number of its major texts which support various tenets of faith.

Anamism is often referred to as man's earliest religion. Yet Nida
and other scholars note that it seems never completely eradicated by any
newly introduced religion that seeks to occupy its place and territory. Instead, many of its more dominant features are assimilated into the new-
comer so that animism continues even though it may have a new mode or
name.[2] Thus animistic concepts and practices are still to be found within
Christianity, Islam, Judaism, Hinduism, Buddhism, etc.

Historians of Southeast Asia say that the Thai people migrated from
their homeland in what is now south China during the twelveth and thirteenth
centuries A. D. Typical of many migrating peoples, they retained many
beliefs and cultural practices of their previous homeland. Also typical of
peoples in a new locale, they adopted and adapted new motifs with which
they became acquainted in the indigenous cultures. These changes were
to be realized in religion, dress, customs and both written and spoken
languages. In spite of the ability to adapt and adjust to the new environment,
the Thai successfully developed their own distinctive style of life and even
formulated their cultural system which still reinforces this living pattern.

Brief Historical Resume: Buddhism reached the area of present-day
Thailand before the Thai peoples did. Legends and historical evidences

---

2. Eugene A. Nida and William A. Smalley, Introducing Animism,
New York, Friendship Press, 1959, pp. 1-3

declare the presence of Buddhism before and about the beginning of the
[3]
Christian Era.   It is quite likely that Buddhism was in this area of Southeast Asia before a definite differentiation between Mahayana and Thera-
[4]
vada as the two vehicles of Buddhism was apparent.   Even when the activiti
of Asoka are omitted, it still appears that King Kanisha of the Punjab, abo
the end of the first century A. D., sent missionaries to China, Tibet and
[5]
Southern China.   Then from Southern India, the Buddhists spread to Srivijaya in Sumatra about 420 A. D. and then into the upper Malay peninsula,
[6]
which was under Srivijaya's control until the twelfth century A. D.   From
here, it also entered the **geographical** areas of southern and central Thailand and gained acceptance by the Mons and Khmers between the first and
[7]
seventh centuries.

Buddhism entered an area already strongly influenced by animism and

---

3. A. L. Basham, The Wonder That Was India, New York, Grove Press
Inc. 1954, p. 56; W. A. R. Wood, History of Thailand, London, Fisher, Uwin,
1926, p. 53; Leon Sinder, "A Brief Sketch of Hinayana Buddhism in Thailan
JOURNAL OF ASIATIC STUDIES, Vol. 7, No 1, 1964, p. 1

4. Sinder, op. cit. p. 1

5. Ibid

6. B. B. Luang, The History of Buddhism in Thailand, Bangkok Chatra
Press, 1955

7. H. G. Q. Wales, Siamese State Ceremonies, Their History and
Function, London, B. Quaritch, 1931, p. 19

affected by Hinduism. Superimposed on a more deeply rooted and pervasive animism, both Buddhism and Hinduism co-existed as intermingling
streams for several centuries.[8] Evidences of Buddhism in Thailand became scarce after the second century A.D., but an inscription at Kedah,
dated in the fourth century A. D., does verify that Buddhism still existed
in the area at that time. Later, the Chinese pilgrim I-Ching wrote that
Buddhism had become prevalent in earlier times than his, but that a
wicked ruler had destroyed it.[9]

Due to Mahayana and non-Buddhist competition during the sixth to tenth
centuries, Hinayana (Theravada) declined in influence in Ceylon.[10] However,
the 11th century King Anurutha of Pagan (Burma) imported bhikkhus from
Ceylon and India in an effort to restore Hinayana to the position which he
believed it deserved.[11] Inasmuch as King Anurutha's conquests included
parts of what is now Thailand, the reintroduction of Theravada is of importance in its historical impact. The imported monks of Ceylon, and the
Tipitakas which they brought with them, were utilized to proclaim the faith
throughout the expanded kingdom of Anurutha's reign.[12]

8. Virginia Thompson, Thailand, The New Siam, New York
9. Kenneth W. Morgan, The Path of the Buddha; Buddhism Interpreted
by Buddhists, New York, Ronald Press, 1956, p. 121
10. Richard A. Gard, Buddhism, Braziller Press, 1962, p. 25
11. John F. Cady, Southeast Asia: Its Historical Development, New
York, McGraw-Hill, 1964
12. Wood, op. cit. pp. 47, 50

The early Thai peoples, coming from northwest China, first settled in south China in the nation-state known as Nab Chao. As the Mongul pressure grew during the 12th and 13th centuries, many Thais emigrated southward into the Southeast Asia area. It is probable that these Thai brought with them some knowledge of Mahayana.[13] Nevertheless, in time, Theravada became the more generally accepted philosophy of religion[14] as the emigrant Thai interacted with such Theravada centers as Sri Thep, Phra Phatom and Phong Tuk in the Menam Basin.[15]

The first Thai dynasty (Pra Ruang) was established in 1238 when two Thai chieftains - Khun Bangklangtao and Khum Pamuang - revolted against the Khmer rule. The successful revolt led to the kingship of Khum Pamuang and a capital being established at Sukhothai .[16] As the dynasty expanded and extended its reign, Sukhothai prospered and Buddhism deepened its cultural roots.

The third king of Sukhothai, Ramkamhaeng (c. 1275-1317),[17] known as

13. Wood, p. 38; Wales, op. cit. p. 14; Sir Charles Eliot, Hinduism and Buddhism, A Historical Sketch, Vol. III, London, Routledge and Kegan Paul, 1857, p. 81; Prince Chula Chakrabongse, "Buddhism In Thailand", Vistas of Thailand, Bangkok, Government Public Realtions Dept, 1963, p. 21

14. Wood, op. cit. p. 38

15. Kenneth P. Landon, Southeast Asia: Crossroads of Religion, Chicago, University of Chicago Press, 1949, p. 102

16. Thailand Official Yearbook of 1964, pp. 13-14

17. G. E. Harvey, History of Burma, London, Longmans, Green and Company, 1925, p. 251

a great ruler, is credited with bring bhikkhus from Nakorn Sritammarat [18] of the Lanka School of Theravada to Sukhothai. These monks, on the Buddhist "sabbaths", preached from the same throne which Ramkamhaeng used to administer the affiars of state on other days. In the eyes of the people, this symbolized the de facto union of "church" and state, and undoubtedly was a factor in persuading some to accept the favored religion. Moreover, Ramkamhaeng arranged and implemented a treaty with Ceylon for other monks to come from Ceylon to reside, preach and teach outside of Sukhothai. For these, the king built the Forest Monastery just west of the capital. A senior monk (Mahathera) was appointed by the king to be the Sangharaja or ruler of the Order of the monks. [19]

King Lithai, ruling from 1355 to 1376, was such a devout Buddhist that he was known as Dhammaraja I, "King of the Law". [20] Even as a vassal of Ayuthia, he was able to secure a senior monk of the Ceylon Lanka Sangha, learned in the Tipitakas, who was received in Sukhothai with the title of Sangharaja. Dhammaraja instituted a number of religious reforms in Thai Buddhism based upon the Pali scriptures which were to the capital at this time.

---

18. Chakrabongse, op. cit. p. 22; also Luang, op. cit.
19. Eliot, p. 43; H. G. Q. Wales, Ancient Siamese Government and Administration, London, B. Quaritch, 1934, p. 241
20. George Coedes, The Making of Southeast Asia, translated by H. M. Wright, Berkeley, University of California Press, 1966, p. 140

Even though the Ayuthia kingdom, founded in 1350 and lasting until the Burmese destroyed it in 1767, replaced that of Sukhothai, Buddhism retained its place as a cultural force of great prestige and honor. King Trailok (also known as Boromotrailokan), who came to the throne in 1448 as a devout Buddhist, invited the Patriarch of the Lanka school to become his royal ordaining Thera.[21]

King Ramatibodi II, son of Trailok who came to the throne in 1491, first established sustained relations with the West through agreements with the Portuguese. He also gave funds for the erection of the first Christian church in his land.[22] However, in 1568-1569, the Burmese captured and sacked Ayuthia, and crowned Mahadhammaraja as the new vassal king. He, in turn, appointed a new Sangharaja to oversee the new Sangha.[23] The appointment of this Sangharaja served to unify the Thai Sangha even though at least two major subgroups existed within it. The first of these two groups, occupied with sacred studies, lived in town-wats and began a series of Buddhist schools. The second group , living in country-side wats, were primarily engaged in meditation, and thereby isolated from much of the daily life experiences of the common peoples of the time.[24]

21. Coedes, Ibid, p. 150
22. Chakrabongse, op. cit. p. 36
23. Wales, Ancient Siamese Government, p. 241
24. Luang, op. cit. p. 30

A few years later, in 1577, the Sangha was divided into Northern and Southern units with provisions made to coordinate help for the poorer wats, and monasteries were ranked according to their importance.[25]

Accounts of the reign of King Narai (1657-1688) show that the Sangha's hierarchy was comparatively embryonic with only the higher ranks of Sangharaja and Tchaou-vat. These alone had the power of ordination of new Sangha members. While no Sangharaja held jurisdiction over other bhikkhus, the one residing at the Royal Palace was the "first among equals".[26] In spite of royal interest at this time, it appears that within the Sangha, the monks handled the inner discipline by Buddhist law rather than by rule of the king.[27]

Under the reign of Mahadhammaraja (Boromakot, 1733-1758), Thai Buddhism attained such status that in 1750 a royal embassy of Ceylon came to Ayuthia to secure Thai monks in order to reform Sinhalese Buddhism. The religion and practice exported by this request was essentially that which had been received many years earlier.

With the fall and destruction of Ayuthia in 1767, organized Buddhism fell into disarray. This disorganization permitted a decline in monastic discipline and permitted a corresponding growth of corruption. King

---

25. Sinder, op. cit. p. 5
26. Wales, Ancient Siamese Government, p. 241
27. Ibid, p. 239

Taksin, who apparently suffered mental deterioration (according to Thai Government histories currently approved and utilized in academic work), was deposed and killed in 1782. Somdech Chao Phya, one of Taksin's generals, as Rama I, became the ruler and founder of the present Chakri dynasty.[28]

Rama I moved the capital from Dhonburi to Bangkok and called a council for the revision of the Tipitaka while also building a special hall to house the revised scriptures.[29] This was then followed by a series of ten royal edicts pertaining to Buddhism between 1782 and 1801. A summary of these reveals the king had decided on drastic procedures for the reformation of Buddhism. Edict One (1782) ordered monks to utilize scripture more in their sermons. Edict Two (1783) redefined the role of the bhikkhu in the community and emphasized the necessity for the Order to follow the two hundred and twenty-seven rules of the Patimokkha. Edicts Three and Four (1783) established requirements for all bhikkhus to carry identification papers issued by the government. Edict Five prescribed governmental penalties for members of the Sangha who were "defrocked" and expelled for violations of the Parajika and handed to governmental courts

---

28. Coedes, op. cit. p. 165; Robert Heine-Geldern, Concept of State and Kingship In Southeast Asia, Ithica, Cornell University Press, 1956, p. 9

29. Thailand Yearbook 1964, p. 21

for additional action.

The sixth Edict (1783) prohibited members of the Sangha from engaging in any occupation or activity considered unworthy while designating both learning and meditation as ideal persuits. The Seventh Edict required the Sangha to prepare lists of all bhikkhus and novices and submit these to the government. While those worthy of commendation were to be called to the attention of the monarch, the disobedient and profligate were to be expelled from the Sangha. This edict closed with the solemn promise:

> Leaders of the monastic units as well as officials of the Department of Church Affairs who neglect their duties by this Edict will be punished.   31

The Eighth Edict emphasized the unity and harmony which ought to exist between the Sangha and the government. It stressed that the government officials would work with the Sangha officials in the promotion of discipline. It also provided channels for royal intervention in the Sangha should disobedient or disloyal monks gain control of its deliberations. [32] The edict listed offenses of the bhikkhus which could range from chess-playing to sexual activities as necessitating royal concern and action.

---

30. Wales, Ancient Siamese Government
31. Ibid,
32. Prince H. H. Dhaninivat, Monarchical Protection of the Buddhist Church In Siam, Bangkok, World Fellowship of Buddhists, 1964. Thus it can be readily seen that the Sangha did not exist as an independent unit in Thailand but as an unit of the state from its early days.

Edict Nine (1794) prescribed procedures for the detection of any bhikkhu who might be guilty of Parajika offenses. The Tenth Edict(1801) ordered the expulsion from the Sangha of those monks who are found guilty of certain offenses. Thus, slowly and surely, the Thai monarch assumed an increasing role in the Sangha's internal affairs. Just as royal interest in the Sangha led to royal decrees and occasional intervention, so it also created the role of financial aid and support. These combined tools could be used as instruments of control if and when needs for such arose.

Another royal prerogative was that of appointing the higher Sangha officials. Perhaps the most classical example was that in which Rama III appointed Prince Mongkut to be the Head of the Pali Examiners when he was only twenty-four years old. Fortunately the Prince was an outstanding scholar, and this position combined with royal rank permitted the future Thai king to establish the reform denomination within Thai Buddhism known as Dhammayutta. The Dhammayutta provided a means for the preaching of adherence to the "original" doctrines of the Buddha within a unified Thai Sangha. While King Mongkut created a number of changes within Thai Buddhism, the key to these can best be seen in the Dhammayut sect or denomination. Even more basic than organizational concepts are the various doctrines vital to Thai Value Systems and Behavior Patterns. Therefore it is proper to briefly look at some of these basic beliefs.

> "There is, there must be, an escape!
> Impossible there should not be!
> I'll make the search and find the way,
> Which from existence shall release!
>
> "Even as, although there misery is,
> Yet happiness is also found;
> So, though indeed existence is,
> A non-existence should be sought. 33

Any meaningful discussion of Thai values and behavior patterns demands knowledge of Buddhism as accepted by Theravadist adherents in Thailand. Most of the Thai cannot give logical explanations of their cultural patterns. (Neither can most Americans of their own culture either!) Nevertheless, both are so accultured by these cultures that certain modes of thinking and acting seem as natural as breathing to them. The same is true of almost any people within their own culture. Yet for an outsider, i. e., a foreigner, observing the culture, the dynamics of such cultural patterns must be under stood if the social mores are to be appreciated. Particularly is this observation relevant when citizens of radically differing cultures are in sustained association as partners striving for mutually agreed objectives.

---

33. Henry Clarke Warren, <u>Buddhism In Translation</u>, New York; Atheneum, 1963 (originally published by Harvard University Press), p. 6, on which the author quotes verses 20 and 21 of the "Story of Sumedha" from the Introduction to the Jataka i, 3i. (The wide number of authors who use the almost exact terminology for Buddhist thoughts preclude listing all of them)

DHAMMA in Pali and Dharma in Sanskrit is one of the Three Jewels

of Buddhism with the other two being the Buddha and the Sangha. As the

teachings of the Buddha and as preserved by the Sangha, the Dhamma

constitutes a basic element of Thai day-to-day psychology. As the Buddha'

earthly existence drew to a close and concern was expressed regarding

a successor, the Buddha is quoted as having said:

"It may be, Ananda, that in some of you the thought might arise:
'the word of the Master is now ended and we have no teacher from
now on.' It is not thus, Ananda, that you should think. For let the
Truth and the Discipline, which I have set forth and laid down for
you all, be your teacher when I am gone." 34

The Dharma means Doctrine, Teaching or Law; and it can
also denote Justice, Righteousness or Natural Law. If anyone
practices the Dharma it means that they are putting themselves
in harmony with Nature and the natural laws which govern the
universe. And the concept in those natural laws is about the
Three Characteristics of life, viz, Anicca, Dukka and Anatta.
All living beings, without exception, are subject to these three
characteristics. They constitute the natural law of the physical
world. Anicca is a summarized statement that in all existences
there is no such thing as permanence. Dukka is that dissatisfact-
ion is involved in life. Anatta means that in all life there is
nothing that can be regarded as psychic substance, thing or "soul".
This is the central doctrine of the Buddha Dharma.   35

---

34. Some Prominent Characteristics of Buddhism , p. 232,"His Noble
Message: Our Teacher By Proxy" in lecture "The Sovereignty of Righteous
ness"; Also confer with Appendix D of this volume for texts and references
as these were placed there to reduce the volume of this study. Appendix
E is a description of the Department of Religious Affairs and the Sangha
as both are significant factors in Thai values and behavior patterns.
35. C. Prabha, Buddhist Holy Days and State Ceremonies of Thailand,
Bangkok, Prae Pittaka Publishing Company, 1964, p. 74

Historically, these doctrines date from the Buddha's first sermon following his enlightenment under the bodhi tree, assattha or ficus religiosa, thought by some Buddhists to be the banyan tree, on the banks of the Neranjara River in Uruvela of present day Gaya.[36] This sermon was that of the "Deer Park" at Benares when he preached the sermon often called "Setting In Motion the Wheel of Dhamma". The central theme of this presentation became the fundamental principles of the Buddha's teachings and include the four basic assertions known as the "Four Noble Truths". It also included other fundamental concepts vital to the development of a "world-view" which has endured and developed during the past twenty-five hundred years. These concepts include the "Three Marks of Existence", which are Impermancy, Unsatisfactoriness and No-Self or as the original language lists them Annica, Dukka and Anatta.

ANNICA is the doctrine of non-permanence, the "Law of Flux" or constant change. Going beyond the scope of life, it applies to everything in the universe. Nothing which takes or has form can endure for eternity. Sooner or later it will be worn away, broken, destroyed or disintegrated and thereby provide material from which new forms come into being.[37]

---

36. Christmas Humphreys, Buddhism, Baltimore, Penguin Books, 1951, p. 16, gives mystical meanings to the term Bodhi by declaring it to be "Bodhi, the Maha Bodi, or Supreme Wisdom, is the purpose of all study, of all morality, of all attempts at self-development."
37. Humphreys, op. cit., p. 17;Khantipalo, op. cit., p. 66;Prabha, op. cit., p. 5.

ANATTA is a natural development of Annica, or the law of change and impermanence. Inasmuch as Annica declares that life is a ceaseless flow of birth, growth, decay and death, Anatta applies to the "soul". Anatta says there is no principle, "soul" or self that is immortal and unchanging. Instead it declares that only the Ultimate Reality is beyond this law. While this life force or "life stuff" may be reincarnated, no personality as such [38] continues to exist after death. Therefore the Buddhists talk of reincarnation rather than the Hindu transmigration. However, in the practice of the more popular forms of Buddhism, this philosophical theme generally appears to be reinterpreted by adherents to mean that they individually will reap the benefits or punishments for deeds performed in this life.

DUKKHA is the First Noble Truth of the Buddha's teaching. This term seems to have no completely satisfactory English equivalent word. Frequently such terms as unsatisfactoriness, imperfection, suffering, etc [39] are used. It seems correct to say that mere existence is Dukkha since this allows, permits and "encourages" less than perfection. Moreover the whole basic thrust of Buddhism is to escape the endless cycle of existence through making sufficient progress to gain Nibbana or the "Void".

---

38. Mole, op. cit., pp. 21, 22; Prabha, op. cit., p. 5; What Is Buddhism?, p. Humphreys, op. cit., p. 17; E. A. Burtt, The Teachings of the Compassionate Buddha, New American Library (A Mentor Classic) 1955, pp. 29-32.
39. The same references as given above apply to Dukkha also.

Birth is sufficient evidence that one has not yet gained Nibbana.

The Second Noble Truth declares that the origin and continuing cause of Existence is "desire" or excessive craving. The Buddha taught that the gratification of what is considered by Westerners as normal drives is really the basic reason that one cannot readily escape this cycle of life and move into Nibbana. In this sense Nibbana cannot be equated with the traditional Protestant Christian concept of heaven by even the wildest imagination. Rather, man's 108 desires, symbolised by the 108 beads of the Buddhist "prayer-beads", must be brought under complete control.

The Third Noble Truth is that dukkha, "existence", comes to an end when all craving and desires cease. Moreover, as there is no transcendant savior, man must bring this about through his own efforts. Until this is achieved, the inherent life force of existence is bound through the endless samsara (wheel of existence) to both endless births and deaths.

The Fourth Noble Truth says that success to Nibbana can come only by following the Eight-Fold Path. Through following this Path, all mankind are provided a way in which they may release themselves from Dukkha - an existence of less than satisfaction - and reach Nibbana. Moreover, as each individual is his own "saviour", he can work out his escape according to his own desires and time reference without regard to the fate of others.

The Eight-Fold Path consists of right understanding, right thought, right speech, right action, right livelihood, right effort, right mindfulness and right concentration.

1. Right Understanding requires awareness of the Buddha's teaching with a thorough self-examination in relation to each of the experiences which one encounters. The Buddha taught that such examinations ought be without self-delusion and rationalization. This would permit each event or emotion to be seen in its true perspective instead of as it appears to be.

2. Right Thought requires sufficient detachment from the idea or event that it might be viewed objectively. Moreover right thought permits one to even examine one's own motive for feelings in regard to others.

3. Right Speech precludes saying anything that may be displeasing about others even though it may be completely true. The application of this teaching through cultures affected strongly by Buddhism explains why foreigners are told what they want to hear rather than the straight hard facts. Thus the Westerner is often faced with a facade which is quite different than reality, but should be accepted and worked through rather than demonstrating impatience, anger or discouragement.

4. Right Action encourages action in harmony with the Buddha's thoughts and teaching. Right action requires the adherent to act quite differently than he may be inclined to do. Certainly right action makes excellent sense in the closed community, and most of Asia is composed of closed communities. The Patimokkha gives the 227 rules of right action and conduct for members of the Sangha.

5. Right Livelihood requires that one's occupation be within the accepted area of earning one's living. It must be one that benefits all living things while avoiding harm to all. It is a practical application of ahimsa, "compassion". This precludes being a killer of animals, a tanner of hides, etc.

6. Right Effort declares that constant practice is required for thought to become or result in the proper development. Thus one must learn to practice self-control, self-appraisal, self-discipline and continuing efforts to understand oneself in light of one's non-being.

7. Right Mindfulness requires that one's total perspective of existence be in focus in daily life. This would permit the individual to relate all thought and actions to reality instead of to the illusions which dominate life.

8. Right Concentration provides sufficient means for the individual to gain insight with its resulting knowledge through deliberate concentration on a single subject. This concept has resulted in the development of several Buddhist schools of thought which utilize varying methods to achieve this goal.

These eight steps are not to be practiced one by one, with success in each one before moving to the next. Instead, they are all closely related and must be simultaneously and continuously practiced. Only in this way can one really aspire to Nibbana. No wonder so many existences are required before one can be free of the Wheel of Existence and gain Nibbana.

THE FIVE PRECEPTS. According to the Buddha, salvation from an ongoing existence is a personal work. The way to Nibbana through the process of Enlightenment is different for each individual due to differing locations on the Wheel of Existence as determined by merits earned or lost in prior existences. Inasmuch as each individual determines, by way of merits and "demerits", their speed or pace toward Nibbana, all rules are basically guidelines to help the individual. Thus the Five Precepts serve as broad markers for human beings outside the Sangha. The extent to which one heeds these is considered to be a matter of one's own choice even though society makes its own feelings on that matter rather strong at times. These Five Precepts or "immoral actions" are (1) Taking Life: (2) Taking what is not given, or stealing; (3) Improper sexual relations; (4) False speech; and (5) Using intoxicants.

The First Precept: Refrain From Taking Life: Since all life is but part of the same Reality, one ought not even take the life of an insect. Of course the Buddhist scriptures have examples of varying degrees of wrongness associated with this offense. One will surely collect unpleasant rewards for wrong deeds while having compassion on all living things will bring forth good rewards.

Second Precept: Refrain from taking what is not given; Don't steal: It is wrong to take advantage of someone's ignorance or misfortune.

34

It is wrong to mistreat anyone for one's own personal gain. Likewise one must not take the property of another by questionable or unscrupulous acts.

Third Precept: Refrain from improper sexual behavior: Basically, this seems to teach that the seeker of Nibbana must have control of sensual pleasures. Thus Sangha members are not supposed to look at a woman, touch her or even ride in a bus seat beside one. The Buddha by precept and example seems to have taught that physical sex relations is less than the ideal standard of conduct for one earnestly seeking Nibbana.

Fourth Precept: Refrain from false speech: The Buddha taught that one should not tell falsehoods even by inference.

Fifth Precept: Refrain from intoxicants and other stimulants which dull the mind: It is considered that the violation of this rule reduces resistence to disobeying the other rules or guidelines.

Buddhists are taught that failure to live in accord with these precepts may jeopardize their status in the next or future incarnations. That is, violation of such precepts may cause them to be reborn in a scale lower than that of human beings, and that Nibbana may be reached only from the level of humanity. Incidentally there are at least five levels of living existence according to the Buddhist dogma, so the foregoing warning is no light matter. Moreover, only through the elimination of ignorance can emancipation within Buddhism become a reality. Since there is no God, saint or intervening power to help man, he must gain his own "salvation".

No one can protect themselves from the results of their own deeds since the impersonal Karmic Law declares that each must suffer or benefit of their own deeds.

Kamma in Pali and Karma in Sanskrit is the law of causality in the ethical sphere. This Law, which is one of action, declares that every effect is produced by some action so that cause and effect are closely related. One sows what they reap so that the present is the child of the past while serving as the parent of the future. In this sense, Kamma is the energy which survives man at death and links this life with those of the past and those of the future. Kamma transmits both the good and bad of the past and present. The good creates favorable conditions even while the bad can lower one's state of existence and prolong one's samsara.

Kamma is another way of saying that every action has a reaction with the doer reaping the benefits be they good or bad. It is predicated upon an ongoing universe which has no superior power to stop it, to speed it up or turn it aside. Thus according to Kamma, there is nothing which can stop or turn aside a particular fate once it has been set in motion. Good actions earn merit while immoral or ignorant actions earn demerits with the latter to be worked out before Nibbana can be achieved.

TIME: The Buddhist concept of time is an endless cycle as symbolized by the Wheel as it has neither beginning nor end. This concept of time, like that of the Hindu, declares that one can move out of time only via Nibbana. This concept of time as an endless repeating cycle makes historical events and significant human epochs incidental to the time span required to reach Nibbana. To the Buddhist philosopher, the world is infinite, without beginning or end, but always changing as it goes through the phases of becoming and unbecoming.[40] This is in contrast to the concept of time as stressed by the Judeo-Christian tradition and accepted by most of the Western World civilizations in recent times.[41]

Reincarnation: According to Buddhism, forms disappear and reappear. Matter never completely disappears, but through an ongoing process rearranges itself and gives birth to a new form. Therefore, man as a part of this natural universe is no exception according to Buddhist dogma. While there is no ongoing "soul", one's life-force is recast into another form and continues until it has run its course and Nibbana is reached. While this is the teaching of the philosopher, most adherents of popular Buddhism think of rebirth as something that will happen to them personally in spite of the philosophical denial of a soul.

---

40. Some Prominent Characteristics of Buddhism, pp. 271-320; What Is Buddhism? p. 55. : Humphreys' Buddhism as a whole; and numerous other writers who all discuss the same subject with general agreement.
41. Robert L. Mole, Vietnamese Time Concepts and Behavior Patterns Charles Tuttle Publishing Company, 1969 (The whole extended discussion).

But even for the philosopher, there appears to be a component of the mind - that aspect or life-force which survives after death - that is a prerequisite for consciousness in again becoming that which is pecular to each individual as he or she have been shaped by actions in previous existences. Accordingly it seems that there is a subconscious identity that Kamma transfers so that its negative or positive results can be worke out in the ongoing generations until it too reaches Nibbana.

Nibbana: Perhaps no single feature of Buddhism is more difficult to be understood by adherents of the historic Protestant Christian faith than this. Unlike the long accepted "Heaven" of Biblical usage, Nibbana is neither a place or even has a fixture in time. Rather it is a state of being that is non-being. It is a transcendence of all emotions, and other feature generally associated with mankind. Eastern writers refer to it as the "Vo" This merely means that it is beyond all sensation and therefore complete liberation.

Realms of Existence: As previously noted, the Buddhists teach that
[42]
there are several realms of existence. Some five or six of these realms exist although only those of the human beings and animals are believed to be perceptible by man under most conditions. The levels are thought to

---

42. What Is Buddhism?, pp. 40-56; The Teachings of the Compassionate Buddha, in various locations; H. C. Warren, Buddhism In Translations, pp 262, 274, 301, 313, 349, 401, etc.

be (1) Hell; (2) Animals; (3) Hungry Ghosts; (4) Titians; (5) Man; and (6) some forms of deities. Each level of existence is continued until the Kammic Law requires either an upgrading or a downgrading depending upon what is inherited from previous existences and what one earns in the present life.

These doctrines are potent forces in the formulation of Thai culture. These continue being influential as they undergird Thai cultural concepts of existence. Some explanation seems to be essential inasmuch as all men seem incurably religious as they attempt to formulate an adequate "world-view". In a very real sense, the drama of man and the story of his religion have been inextricably intertwined. In fact, one of the basic functions of religion appears to be that of a cultural gyroscope as it seeks to provide a stable set of definitions of the world in relation to the individual self. These definitions in turn permit the individual or society meet the tran-science and crises of life with some equanimity. Thus, religion, whatever its name or form, constitutes one of the strongest of cultural determinants. The following chapters will explore just how these belief systems mold Thai culture and how this in turn has control of behavior patterns seen
43
throughout Thailand.

---

43. In addition to the cited authorities, on-site research permitted an almost unlimited contact with both Thai and foreign experts on Thai Buddhism. Among the latter not formally listed was Thomas C. Wyatt, American scholar who has been a Thai Buddhist monk; Dr. Richard Gard; etc.

CHAPTER III

THAI STUDENT VALUES

Education is an integral part of the socio-economic development of contemporary Thailand. The 1960 National Education Plan
envisioned the expansion of compulsory education to seven years
by 1980. The development of adequate facilities and staff are
essential if this goal is to be reached. These will require extensive
enlargement of buildings, staffs and college student bodies in view
of Thailand's rapidly growing population.

The last year for which accurate figures are available is 1966.
Figure (A) shows the existing school plans and enrollment with
the target goals for 1971. Figure (B) demonstrates the ratio of
Thai students to the total population within certain age groups, and
appears to indicate that approximately twenty five percent of the
potential student enrollment is not now in school. Figure (C) is
a cost breakdown of the amount spent for education per student for

each academic level from primary through the university. [1] Figures of this latest official report also reveal that only six per cent of the students completing elementary education continue their secondary education. This is to say that out of 4,527,000 only 380,351 continue their formal education beyond the seventh grade. Only 1.55 of the population of college age are in a college or university for a total of 33,961 students in secular colleges and universities when the military schools are not included. [2]

In a non-progressive nation, this number of graduates might suffice to maintain the nation's essential needs. But this number is insufficient for a rapidly developing nation with an exploding population. Thailand recognizes the seriousness of her problem and through the National Plan is taking corrective action.

The values of this comparatively limited number of students are very important due to the small percentage of adult Thai that do have a higher education. In practical terms, these students are the potential builders, educators, administrators and molders of values held by the

---

1. Special Report: Evaluation of Thailand's Economic Development- Development of Education, BANGKOK WORLD, 9 May 1968, p. 21- confer page 42 - of this paper for figures A, B, C.

2. Ibid,

DEVELOPMENT OF EDUCATION UNDER THE FIRST PLAN AND TARGETS FOR 1971

EDUCATION LEVEL	EXISTING ENROLMENT (1966)			ENROLMENT IN 1971		
	STUDENT	TEACHER	SCHOOL	STUDENT	TEACHER	SCHOOL
PRIMARY (PRATHOM 1-7)	4,768,000	152,133	27,939	5,504,000	213,851	29,087
GENERAL SECONDARY (MS 1-5)	345,502	11,517	1,500	575,700	21,560	1,716
VOCATIONAL SECONDARY	42,500	5,650	187	63,000	8,200	200
TEACHER TRAINING	19,776	1,898	30	31,700	2,533	32
ADVANCED TECHNICAL	8,480	884	9	19,090	2,009	10
UNIVERSITY	33,531	2,247	7	43,630	3,500	9

FIGURE A

■ POPULATION □ STUDENT

AGE 19-23
TOTAL 2,191,000 — 1.55%

AGE 17-19
TOTAL 1,877,000 — 5.99%

AGE 14-16
TOTAL 2,150,000 — 12.69%

AGE 14-18
TOTAL 4,027,000 — 9.43%

AGE 7-13
TOTAL 6,262,000 — 76.33%

FIGURE B

UNIVERSITY TOTAL 33,961

HIGHER SECONDARY (MS 4-5)
TOTAL 105,050

LOWER SECONDARY (MS 1-3)
TOTAL 270,720

COMBINED SECONDARY
TOTAL 380,351

PRIMARY (PRATHOM 1-7)
TOTAL 4,779,870

1966 PER CAPITA GOVERMENT EXPENDITURE
ON STUDENTS AT DIFFERENT LEVELS
OF EDUCATION

	BAHT
PRIMARY	278
GENERAL SECONDARY	888
VOCATIONAL SECONDARY	3,528
TEACHER TRAINING	4,278
UNIVERSITY	19,504

FIGURE C

42

vast majority of the following generation as their education makes them influential in whatever role they occupy. Three student bodies not listed in the educational figures just quoted are those in military schools, in the two Buddhist Sangha universities and the Thais enrolled abroad in foreign educational institutions.[3]

The oldest secular university in Thailand is Chulalongkorn which was founded in 1910 by King Chulalongkorn as a school for Royal Pages. In 1911 King Vachirvut changed it into the Civil Service School with it being designated as a university in 1917. Originally founded to educate the elite of Thai culture, it is still the most prestigious school in the country.

In 1934 Thammasat, the second secular school, was established as the University of Moral and Political Science. It was and is basically a university "of, by and for" Thailand's civil service. Traditionally, it has furnished the nation with Governors, District Officers, lawyers, judges and other political figures.

---

3. Confer Robert L. Mole, The Role of Buddhism In the Contemporary Development of Thailand as reprinted for Navy Personal Response COMNAVSUPPACT Saigon FPO 96626, pp. 88-92 for A discussion of the Buddhist Universities

The third non-church-related university to be founded was established as the University of Agriculture in 1943 by an act of Parliment. Since then, it has expanded into other areas of human knowledge as it continues to grow into the status of a major university. In 1943 the Medical School of Chulalongkorn became a separate entity as the University of Medical Sciences. Then in the same year of 1943 a third school, the School of Fine Arts, was changed into the University of Fine Arts.

Chiengmai University recently became the first of Thailand's universities to be located in the provinces. This has been quickly followed by one called Khon Khaen with still another being established for the southern part of Thailand called the Prince of Songkhla University. Thus, there are eight secular universities in Thailand beside the two Buddhist Sangha Universities of Mahachulalongkorn and Mahamakut. [4] Besides these schools, Thailand has thirteen teacher training colleges with four being in Bangkok; two in the South; two in the North; four in the Northeast, and one in Central Thailand outside of Bangkok. Lastly, there are a few

---

4. Ibid; Also see Appendix E, section (a) Education in "Organized Dissemination of Buddhism"

technical institutions which like the military academies offer professional education for careers in well defined areas.

It is difficult to discuss the "values" of Thai university and college students as the term does not lend itself to an easy translation or documentation. Apparently, Alan E. Guskin's Changing Values of Thai College Students[5] is still the best available scientific study in the area. Guskin worked with the encouragement, cooperation and support of Chulalongkorn to scientifically administer a carefully prepared questionnaire to 1,324 males and 1,554 females for a total of 2,878 students in nine colleges, Chulalongkorn and Medical Universities.[6] Many of the values, opinions, beliefs and attitudes of students are complex, difficult to trace and often based on elusive feelings not always subject to conscious analysis. Yet these are the values, beliefs and standards accepted as legitimate. Their declarations thereby constitute an important set of social facts besides being analyzable as possible determinants of cultural dynamics.

---

5. Alan E. Guskin, Changing Values of Thai College Students, Bangkok, Faculty of Education, Chulalongkorn University, 1964

6. Ibid, pp. 1-6

Guskin ascertained that the vast majority of the students come from families with incomes of less that 5,000 Bahts (a Thai Baht can be safely computed to be equal to an American nickel) or 250 American dollars per month. 58.4 per cent come from families who earn less than one hundred dollars a month. [7] Even these figures seem high when measured against the per capita income of Thai farmers who are reputed to earn 500-600 Baht per year. [8] Nevertheless, many students come from farm families with some 43.2 per cent in Provincial colleges, 38.1 per cent in Bangkok colleges with the two tested universities bringing down the average to 28.1 per cent of the total student body questioned. [9]

It is obvious that higher education is greatly respected in Thailand. Middle class and poorer families often make real sacrifices to educate their children. Pride in having a child in the University seems to exceed even the pride of owing a new automobile, a nice house or social standing for the parents. "In general the financial status of the girls' families is higher than

7. Ibid, p. 14

8. "Rice and Farmers", BANGKOK WORLD, 18 May 1968, p. 12

9. Guskin, op. cit. p. 17

that of the boys' families".[10] It also seems that only the exceptional

provincial student can compete against those of Bangkok for a place

in the universities. This is largely due to the current poorer facilities

of the rural areas, but these are being upgraded constantly. However,

once the rural lads are in the colleges and universities, the poorer

men seem to excell as they are diligent and highly motivated.

Undoubtedly they are well aware that should they fail in school, their

choice of life occupations will be limited to farming or entering the

cities' expanding non-specialized work-forces. Few of the students

hold part time jobs so they have to receive either scholarships or

support from family, etc. The only exceptions to this observation

would be those in the Buddhist universities and the military schools.

    The university world in which they live is a secularized world.
The number of young men going into the priesthood in a rural village may, according to one study, exceed 76 per cent. The number
of young men in the university who have been, or plan to go into
the priesthood, is so low as to be almost unmeasurable. (The
Buddhist University excepted, of course). The students are interested in vocation, in technology, in science. They are at least as
materialistic as those whose materialism they may sometimes
decry. This cannot be harmonized with Buddhism. It should not
be attempted. Kukrit Pramoj, himself, has pointed out that the
whole concept of economic development runs counter to Buddhism.
Somehow Buddhism will have to adjust. The students are not about

---

10. _Ibid_, p. 14

47

to give up their electric guitars for bamboo flutes. They are
not about to give up western movies they love for Thai classical
drama. If you have any doubt, go stand by the ticket selling
booths.

The Thai student is avidly learning all he can about western
science and technology, especially in so far as it may contribute
to his comfort or well-being. He is not interested in philosophical discussion. He is passionately interested in "progress".
He is Buddhist because a "good" Thai is Buddhist. But Buddhism
and nationalism are only engaged to be married. They are not
finally and permanently "one flesh".[11]

What do these students want most? They want good jobs with

good pay. They want status and most of all they place the highest

value on security. Many prefer to accept a government position

which offers security and status to accepting a business role which

involves some risk even though the latter may offer opportunities

for much greater income.[12] However, Dr. Brohm of the International

Institute of Education points out that while the last ten years have

seen the number of Thai students going to America double, the

numbers now studying Business Administration have quadrupled.

This, then, seems to be a trend away from civil service "status"

preparation toward pragmatic goals of money-making.[13]

---

11. Ray C. Downs, "Changing Thai University Student Attitudes",
Mimeographed paper of 19 May 1968, p. 3 (Bangkok, Thailand, Bangkok
Christian Student Center Manager).

12. Ibid, pp. 3-4; Guskin, op. cit. 24-53

13. Downs, op. cit. p. 4

48

Generally, Thai women in the colleges or universities were more "security conscious" than the men. This may be because of the scarcity of opportunities for women in comparison to men. It was also true that the university students seem to be more "money-oriented" or motivated toward money-making occupations than are the students of Teacher Training Colleges. This could be due to a sense of realism by the college students; it could be due to a greater exposure of material advantages secured by money to those living in the city; or it could be due to the greater exposure to Buddhist teachings by the rural students who come from villages where the wat is still the center of activities.

The Thai educational institutions type the students into the profession for which they will train. Thus, it is of value to understand why students choose their particular area of study. This also provides an insight into their value system. The students involved in Guskin's study divided themselves into future teachers, doctors, natural scientists, farmers, government officials and business people. The students see their future roles as:

FUTURE TEACHERS: The boys see their future occupation in terms of security and their ability to be useful to others. The girls are mainly concerned with the same qualities, but in the reverse order ....

FUTURE DOCTORS:	Both boys and girls are most interested with being useful to others and independence with girls also concerned with security.
FUTURE NATURAL SCIENTISTS	Boys are most concerned with independent work and special ability, girls with security and secondly with being useful to others and independent work.
FUTURE FARMERS:	Both boys and girls are overwhelmingly concerned with independent work and somewhat less with security.
FUTURE BUSINESS PEOPLE	Both boys and girls are concerned with independent work and security - the boys choosing independent work first, the girls choosing security first.
FUTURE GOVERN- MENT OFFICIALS	(Only boys) they are concerned very strongly with security, and to a much lesser degree with being useful to to others or using special abilities. [14]

It is well to remember the expectation that one's chosen career will gratify certain values may create the very conditions which can transform the wish into reality. Thus, these images can have real consequences for the values "really" predominant in each profession. Particularly is this true if they serve to funnel into each field, young people whose occupational values correspond to those values they think characterize the career they have selected. [15]

---

14. Guskin, op. cit. pp. 34-35

15. Rose K. Goldsen, M. Rosenberg, R.M. Williams, Jr., E.A. Suchman, What College Students Think, Princeton: D. Van Nostrand Co; 1960, p. p. 45-6

Traditionally, the abbot of the wat, the headmaster of the school and the village headman have been thought to be the most important people of the community. It is of interest, therefore, to note how the students rank occupations in relationship of their importance to one another. Both men and women tended to agree on the listing with the exception of the last two positions. Listing from most important down, both men and women ranked the teacher as first, then doctor, priest, soldier, government official, farmer, merchant. The men then listed laborer as higher than royalty outside the King's immediate family while the girls reversed this order. This particular student study showed that the medical students rated the doctor as first and the teacher second while the government student listed the government official as most important. [16]

A commonly discussed characteristic Thai quality is the desire to be free of supervision and to be independent. [17] While this is in total accord with the Buddha's teaching, it appears inconsistent with Thai social structure which maintains a rather strict code of behavior in

---

16. Guskin, op. cit. pp. 36-38

17. David Wilson, Politics In Thailand, Ithaca, Cornell University Press, 1963

superior-subordinate relationships. For instance, in this code a subordinate is never expected to contradict his superior as the latter is credited with being knowledgable in his position. Moreover, subordinates become rather dependent on the superior in private life as well as on the job. Yet beneath a surface submission there seems to be a striving or longing for independent action and freedom from restriction. The students tend to judge relationships between occupations. While their evaluations may appear to be unrealistic, this is what they perceive. This is the way they see reality and it is their perceptions and feelings which will influence them in the future in whatever roles they occupy.

Idealistically the students chose intelligience and ability as the most important qualities in securing employment. Next to these, they listed perseverance with only a few including "knowing the right people" or having family influence and connections.[18] It may be that they should have also included goal-setting as this is one of the most important elements in being motivated to act. If these students measure up to their ideal concepts of the roles they have chosen for themselves, many of them will be rather energetic in

---

18. Guskin, p. 45

their future employment. However, attitudes are only one important influence on the actual behavior of individuals. Strong societal factors must also be considered. The young Thai may wish to marry for "love", romance, etc, but other pressures may create a marriage for financial or social status reasons under parental influence. And obedience to elders is one of the earliest lessons all Thai youth are taught. Thus, most Thai youths raised in a culture where obedience is highly valued, tend to unconsciously conform needs and desires to those of their elders. As this occurs, the suitability factors of money, status, influence, etc., may outweigh "love", understanding or other emotional factors. Thus, the Thai student, like all other people , has both self-images and real-images which do not always agree. The self-image may be a reflection of internal desires while the real image is often the result of internal desires strongly influenced or controlled by external pressures. Scientific analysis reveals that the self-image and the real-image are in harmony only infrequently.

Perhaps the key to understanding Thai students and their value-belief-behavior systems is an awareness and appreciation of the differences and interplay between internal desires and external behavior. Certainly this is essential for an appreciation of Thai social relationships. People in Thailand seem to always operate on two distinct conscious levels-one is their feelings and desires while the other is their external behavior. Thai society places very great value on external signs of respect and subservience on the part of subordinates and students are always in this category except to those below them in age and learning.

One of the basic tenets of Thai society is that all social relationships must be happy, pleasant, smooth and not contain any overt conflict. Whether or not one likes another person, he is to treat that individual courteously. Smiling is not only a gesture toward one's friends, but toward all people. In many ways Thailand is a land of smiles - on the surface. But no people, as a nation, are always happy; no people as a collective whole, are always relaxed or are necessarily expressing good feelings by their smile. It is therefore necessary to understand people on a deeper level than merely their surface external behavior patterns.

Generally, however, it is safe to presume that the present generation of Thai college students have set for themselves certain definite goals. These are usually fairly immediate goals, generally quite materialistic, and include the concepts of "progress" and "success". They, therefore, demonstrate an impatience not always seen in the population of Thailand or even in the parents of the students. In spite of this fact, there is not the alienation from

54

the preceding generation which is evident in America and Europe. The Thai college student is not deeply involved in a search for personal identity. He does not seem afflicted with a doubt as to where he is going, nor do serious misgivings of social values create overwhelming concern. Generally, the five-pronged motto of Chulalongkorn, "Seniority, Order, Tradition, Unity, Spirit", is accepted without any conscious or overt conflict. [19] As long as these offer security, no objection will be raised by the students since they consistently give the highest value to "security" in determining life's work and its methods.

Family is still very important to Thai students in spite of their "loosely structured society". But even this is based on its economic and security values in much the same way that the students look at grades and degrees. Generally, the value of grades is limited to their usefulness in securing a degree. A degree, in turn, is important, but basically because it offers a doorway to jobs, pay, status and above all, security. Other student attitudes include those favoring population control, respect for the United States power, fear of Red China's long-range goals, etc. But all these latter points are secondary to one's individual involvement with life. Student values-beliefs-attitudes and

---

19. Downs, op. cit. p. 5

behavior are being affected by Westernized educational concepts and
exposure to realms of information and knowledge unknown to most
Thai. Therefore, the next chapter discusses beliefs-values and
behavior as seen throughout Thailand modified by varying economic
and geographical differences within the nation.

CHAPTER IV

REAL BEHAVIOR

It is of value to recall that attitudes, which affect behaviorisms,
consist of three separate components which are interlocked with
each other. The first of these is the emotional or affective aspect
of attitude which is descriptive of the "feelings" involved in the
particular attitude. The second factor is the cognitive aspect or
the information and knowledge that one has about the particular
subject and its relationship to other pertinent areas. The third
aspect is the behavioral or tendency of the individual to move
toward the object of his attitude.[1] These three factors provide an
additional re-inforcement of the necessity to understand belief-

---

1. A detailed explanation of these three aspects may be found
in Daniel Katz and Ezra Stotland, "A Preliminary Statement To a
Theory of Attitude Structure and Change" in Sigmund Kock (Editor)
Psychology: A Study of a Science, New York, McGraw Hill, 1959,
Vol. III, pp. 428-432.

value systems of any people if there is a desire to appreciate behavior patterns when these differ in any aspect from those to which the observer is accustomed.

Religion was and still is to a major extent the keystone of Thai culture. Cosmological and astrological beliefs dictate the concept and form of the governmental structure, rituals, and affect the timing of most human activities. The concepts of supernatural power and deities continue to affect human relations, religious and agricultural rituals and the arts. Buddhist code determines the ethical and moral systems, influences the belief in an "afterworld", largely dominates literature, and until quite recently, architecture also. While Buddhist religious beliefs may be reinterpreted and institutions changed, the core concepts seem to remain largely intact.

In many important respects, the Thai value system is inseparable from the Thai version of Thevarada Buddhism. Thus, an awareness of Thai Buddhist beliefs and practices can provide insights for Thai values and behavior. The cycle of life of all status groups in Thai society revolves directly or indirectly about activities associated with Buddhism since almost every community has its Buddhist temple and its monks. The foregoing is true although "Buddhism and animism are intimately fused in the Thai

58

heart"[2]

It is imperative that foreign observers understand the pervasive influence of the yellow-robed monks if valid appreciation of Thai behavior is to be a reality. It is doubted that any Western culture has anything which might be compared to the role which these monks have in the life of Thailand insofar as the majority of its people are concerned. A foreigner, who became a Buddhist monk and then renounced his Buddhist beliefs, in discussing the Angha, declares, "Buddhist monks in Thailand preserve their celibacy to an admirable, an incredible degree"[3]. The same Westerner insists the reason that this can be done so well is that the monks, due to animistic influences, know themselves to be more than men, not in moralistic or rational terms, but in magical terms. [4] According to him, this is in part an outgrowth of the term "Phra" which in Thailand means several things. While the dictionary defines the term as "excellent", it has additional Thai flavoring for the King is "phra" as are Buddhist monks, images and

---

2. Michael A. Wright , "Some Observations on Thai Animism", PRACTICAL ANTHROPOLOGY, Jan-Feb. 1968, p.1

3. Ibid, p.7

4. Ibid

amulets. In popular Buddhism, by the symbolic and ritualistic death at ordination, the monk is no longer mere man, but "phra" among his fellow Thai. In one sense this term is comparable in Thai thought to "Emmanuel" in Christian theology where it is "God with us". Through the ordination rite, the intangibles of the Dhamma become personified, so that the monks are the visible evidences of the intangible Power behind all existence just as the Incarnate Jesus symbolizes the Trinity for Christians. It is this thought that provides the basis for the belief that offerings presented to monks have been given directly to the Supreme Power so that their value is greatly enhanced. [5]

Many of the values of the Thai value-behavior system may be found in other Buddhist and non-Buddhist countries also. The significant point to note here is that Theravadist teachings and the Thai value system have matched each other so well until now. The Thai value system tends to center around personal values rather than national or political values so that some conflict with nationalism may develop. Generally their value system requires

---

5.   Wright, op. cit. pp. 1-7

extremely little commitment or obligation toward other individuals or institutions. This is in harmony with Buddhist teachings regarding the responsibility of each individual to work out his or her own salvation, "Kamma". Likewise the stress placed upon self-reliance and avoidance of involvement, attachment or emotional commitments is not only a part of the Buddhist ethical system but an integral part of the Thai value system.

Regardless of philosophical concepts, most Thai seem to believe in kamma, reincarnation, "Do good, receive good; Do evil, receive evil", etc. Such beliefs are reflected behaviorally by the preoccupation of all rural Thai and many urban dwellers, including many Western-educated ones, with forms of merit-making so that their kamma might be improved. This concern with merit and kamma cannot be ignored in the evaluation of Thai value-behavior patterns since so many activities from the cradle to the grave are intimately connected with it. While many Thai do not expect an immediate Nibbana, they do seem to hope for more concrete rewards in this or the next existence. This more limited view of Kamma does not seem to detrimentally affect the form or intensity of Thai merit-making. Merit-making is the personal concern, privilege and obligation of each individual toward himself or herself rather than to any divine or secular authority. The fact that someone holds a higher status within Thai society is often interpreted by numerous Thai as simply meaning that their kamma is better and that through merit earned in previous existences, they have earned this position.

Thailand has a well defined social stratification with little social equality demonstrated or expected. It is a society which seems to greatly prize its superior-subordinate distinctions in both formal and informal relations. These are so fixed that few Thai have an equal. Almost everyone is older or younger, superior or subordinate. Even twins born a few moments apart are younger and older brother or sister as the case may be. This need to clearly identify the proper role of another, and of one toward another, requires strangers to quickly and astutely ascertain the proper roles before anything except the most inconsequential conversation can ensue.

Such a social structure readily lends itself to the military system of administration for military rank differentials become respected as they easily identify the superior-subordinate roles. They also reinforce social stratification created by cultural training. A second reinforcement is gained through the Thai universal military training program as all Thai males, except the practicing monks, have military training involving courtesy, customs and discipline. Possible negative factors contributing to this stratification may be the limited number of Thai who have sufficient education to effectively challenge the system, and the Buddhist doctrines urging non-involvement in much of life due to its illusionary features.

By virtue of the rigidly-structured social system and the contribution which official rank gives to it, the King bestows military rank upon various government officals. Many have never been in military service nor do they have any intention of being there in a military role. This practice of bestowing rank aids the Thai to more quickly ascertain the proper superior-subordinate role deemed essential by language and social customs. Even the Sangha is marked by rank as signified by fans, gift-boxes, satchels and special names for each grade or level within the Sangha. It is also designated by seniority within the Sangha which may be observed in ceremonies through the relative positions which the monks occupy to one another as the junior ones are always to the rear of a group gathered in ritual.

In spite of such social stratification, Dr. William Bradley insists that equalitarianism is a definite fact of Thai life. This appears to be impossible as social stratification and equalitaranism are in contrast normally. Bradley argues that the sense of equality is another

63

of Buddhism's contributions to the Thai. He says:

Now, another of the very important influences besides the
idea of order is equalitarianism. I think this is probably a
better term than democracy. Really, I do not believe that
Westerners really understand the Thai idea of democracy as
they call it and we in the West cannot believe in our hearts that
you can have a military oligarchy or a dictatorship in a country
and still the people say they are living in a democratic society.
And yet in this society, there is a very definite equalitarianism
and it comes to this country through Buddhism. Many scholars
have pointed out the fact that you have two elements in the
political ideals of a country. The one is the paternalistic idea
of monarchy which is authoritarian with authority always coming
from the top down, and on the other hand, you have the idea
that every person is equal to every other person as a person.
This makes for an amazing amount of social mobility. Here is
the descendent of a King who is being phased out of nobility.
Each generation a little less royalty adheres to a nobleman.
But on the other hand, a person who wants to go to a university
here must take an entrance examination and it matters not
whether he belongs to a rich family or poor, is a nobleman or
not, if he cannot pass the examination, he will not be admitted
to the University. As a result, if his family has money they
will send him to a foreign university and they ask no questions
and he .gets a good education anyway. But this is a democratic
element in the Thai social structure, the idea of equalitarianism.
Buddhism broke the caste system in India and where you have
Buddhism you have this notion that every person has the same
opportunity for Nipon - release - that there are no priviledges
for people because of their social or economic standing. [6]

---

6. Dr. William Bradley, "The Influence of Buddhism On
Society and Education in Thailand", Lecture manuscript for the
East-West Center in Bangkok 1965, p. 3 (Copy of undated lecture
for symposium at East-West Center provided to this writer by
Mrs. Murchie, Director for the Center.

Because Thai culture has this factor of equalitarianism, based upon basic Buddhist beliefs, the role of the individual in Thailand often baffles the foreign observer who may have a contrasting cultural mold.

INDIVIDUALISM: The self-image of the Americans is often that of the unique individual who stands on his own feet, fighting his own battles and winning against overwhelming odds. Nevertheless, the qualities of individuality displayed in Thailand makes the American appear rather cultural-bound by external pressures. The Thai individual's role in society seems different from that of other Asian countries even when factors of Buddhism are considered. Some sovereign states are basically composed of peoples bound together by common ideals, geography, etc. as primary forces of union; some seem to be based informally or formally upon tribal cohesion; others, like Vietnam, seem to be basically family-oriented. The Thai social structure appears to be predicated primarily upon the individual.

John Embree declared that Thai society is divergent from all other Asian societies and designated it as a "loosely-structured social system"[7]. A Thai folk-saying expresses the same thought by declaring, "One who can do as one likes is a genuine Thai".

---

7. John Embree, "Thailand - A Loosely-structured Social System", American Anthropologist, (1950) LII, pp. 181-193

Herbert Phillips in his excellent study, <u>Thai Peasant Psychology</u>, stressing the Thai quality of individuality notes that the Thai social system is based upon the theme "that relations between people should be friendly, genial and correct, but need little personal commitment or involvement".[8] It is this readiness to phrase all face-to-face encounters in social rituals with little or no commitment that lies at the base of Embree's terminology "loosely-structured social system". Phillips declares emphatically, "Siamese are, first and foremost, free and independent souls. Much of the time they fulfill each other's expectations, but this is only because they want to, not because others expect it of them or because the situation demands it".[9] The potentialities for excessive or unbearable interpersonal frustrations in such an individualistic society are minimized by the seasoned hesitation to have strong expectations about events or people. Phillips points out that the results are most Thai rarely live at, or even reach, a high

---

8. Herbert P. Phillips, <u>Thai Peasant Psychology</u>, Berkeley, University of California Press, 1966, p. 55

9. <u>Ibid,</u> p. 60

emotional pitch.[10]

Buddhism stresses the individuality of each life force until it achieves Nibbana. Each person is solely responsible for his or herself. This may be the major reason that Thailand has so few voluntary organizations outside of the specialized professional, economic or cultural ones patterned largely on Western values. Dr. Bradley in discussing Thai individualism notes:

> You are responsible for yourself and you must take responsibility for your own life and your own decisions. This is a form of enlightened self-interest. On the other hand, you have a sensitivity to the other person which is usually lacking in our Western culture. You know Christians and Jews are taught that, "you are your brother's keeper", and this is taken for granted as a very good thing. Here they are taught that you are not your brother's keeper and there must be some social distance between you and the other person and you preserve his right to be free from your interest, from your prying concern, from being seen by you. So there is this notion of forebearance. You do not interfere with another person, not because you are not interested in him, but because you have no business interferring with him. It is for him, not you, to make his decision.[11]

Undoubtedly, some would be inclined to think that the foregoing is more diplomatic than factual. Nevertheless, it does convey the sense of individual isolation from involvement with other persons so that

---

10. Ibid, p. 60

11. William Bradley, op. cit pp. 3-4

one acts as he or she believes best for them rather than for the good of the community at a personal loss.

Unlike ancient Israel in the time after Joshua when anarchy resulted when "every man did that which was right in his own eyes"[12], Thai society functions quite well in spite of its prominent individualistic orientation. Relationships with other people are characterized by a large measure of reciprocity. I do something for you with the expectation that you will do something for me in return. If I discover that you are not doing that something for me, I will no longer feel any obligation to execute what I had been expected to do for you. Additionally the rural villagers' sense of hierarchy, superior-subordinate status and mutually dependent requirements are fairly keen. Such patterns of cooperation are essential in the necessary tasks of village life. These are pragmatic, reliable and workable because they meet the need of all who are involved.[13]

INDIVIDUAL ATTITUDE AND BEHAVIOR TOWARD AUTHORITY:

The Thai seem to accept authority with much less obvious tension

---

12. Judges 17:6 (King James Version of the Holy Bible)

13. Confer Konrad Kingshill, RU DAENG - The Red Tomb, A Village Study in North Thailand, Bangkok, Bangkok Christian College, 1965.

than do Americans. There is always deference, courtesy and proper status respect formally expressed toward those in authority over the individual. Normally the wisdom or competence and efficiency of the authority figure is not too openly questioned. However if the authority figure does not honor the accepted reciprocal relationships, the oppressed individual may simply quietly cease to follow higher directions. This latter course will be done without rudeness, discourteousness or any public display of indignation.

Passiveness in regard to authority seems to be an acceptable solution to the Thai who accept the concept of power as a by-product of virtue, or Buddhist Merit. The higher the individual status is within the Thai social hierarchy, the greater his piety and wisdom are thought to be. Even when misuse of power occurs, the Thai with faith in cosmic retribution is supposed to remain undisturbed - after all tyrants can be reborn as dogs while those who are abused by tyranny are not really martyrs. Instead, they are persons who must work out their Kamma due to misdeeds of their previous existences. Since power comes from an unknowable source, its effectiveness is the major criterion for judging its magnitude.

The Thai peasant is largely concerned with his immediate world and not too concerned about events beyond his horizon. Moreover, he tends to ignore or not question matters beyond his ability to influence or control them. This attitude may help to explain why there is no history in which the Thai peasant has revolted in class warfare. Of the twenty-seven coups since the 1932 coup d'etat established the constitutional monarchy, none have directly involved the peasantry. Instead, they have been the reshuffling of key figures within the powerful elite near the top of Thailand's government.

The dispassionate view of the world by many peasants and their historic disinterest in "political solutions" can be either an advantage or disadvantage of the Royal Government in its counter-insurgency activities. At present, it seems that their will to resist insurgents stems from their desire to be left alone more than it does a sense of loyalty. This results in a passive resistance much more frequently than it does in an active participation in "national defense".

The government is aware of this, and is now involved in promoting a sense of national identity through the mass media; by colorful pictures of the King and Queen, the Buddha and the Supreme Patriarch; by expanding and improving the educational system; by utilizing members of the Sangha as missionaries in largely non-Buddhist areas, and by intensive rural development. All these efforts are carefully orchestrated for maximum value due to the

70

structure of the royal government. Thai governmental power is skillfully distributed, dispersed and diluted with the real authority emanating from the top. This may seem rather dictatorial and even as an imperious autocracy to Americans, but it appears to generally meet the needs of Thailand. It also harmonizes with the general concept that power, prestige, wealth and authority are the results of karmic law, so who is mere man to thwart the immutable law?

Moreover, most Thai are aware that parallel to the formal structure of government is an informal one. An understanding of its existence and how it operates is essential to foreigners within Thailand if they are to have insights into the realities of Thai life. Only the naive limit their knowledge to governmental structure charts embossed with seals. Generally the rural Thai are accustomed to being told what to do in secular life by the village headman or teacher while the monks attend to his spiritual affairs. This of course is subject to change as modernization becomes a reality in their small communities even though these may be well off the beaten path.

One may expect to see the social culture of an area reflected by its members and institutions so that some predication of behavior of individuals and institutions are possible. By understanding the impinging and influencing forces of the social cosmos, it is possible to anticipate what behavior patterns will be determinative. No organization is able to strip away in a matter of months - or years depending on the date of action onset - the individual's cultural laminate applied by a society during his formative years. This socialization process leaves its indelible mark on the individual as he or she become a product of that society.

When a society has a membership imbued with the social ways which are being described for Thailand, it naturally follows that such a society must have adequate leadership stimulus if effective operations are to occur. When this leadership is absent, no action will be taken. This is so strongly ingrained that effective social change in Thailand needs the sanction of the King or the Prime Minister. Even so simple a matter as a two cent bus fare raise in Bangkok in May 1968 could not be finalized until the Prime Minister returned from abroad and gave the final decision.[14]

The Thai seem to expect their leaders to be benevolent regardless of rank distance be it in the government, military or social life. Leaders are aware of this expectation and generally conform

_____

14. Author's on-site observation and as recorded in the BANGKOK WORLD during the month of May 1968.

to this expectation. Leaders are likewise expected to act calmly, in a self assured manner as they exercise their authority. Moreover, as these leaders occupy a certain authority position, no one below that level may challege the decisions made by the one holding this position. Disinclination, nay, prohibition against criticism - coupled with religious taboos of wrong speech and equanimity - disallow sanctions for mild mal practice or even no practice at all. Generally the Thai is culturally pressured to leave things as they are and refrain from speech or action that may imply criticism. This same social pressure is exerted to keep him on his level and not attempt to assume authority on a higher social, governmental or military level.

In fact the Thai word CHAI YEN, "Cool Heart", describes an ideal of the Thai. To have a cool heart is to be uninvolved, not annoyed and to remain in control of one's emotional self. With a cool heart one avoids unhappy situations and takes whatever pleasure is available from each circumstance or situation. To best do this, one of the basic rules of Thai behavior is to avoid face-to-face-conflicts. Coolness is a visible attitude expressing freedom from agitation, denoting one's capacity to transcend temptations of conflict, aggression, greed, outbursts of enthusiasm or discouragement. Being cool does not imply that life has no threat, anxiety, temptation or difficulty. Instead it marks a posture by which one conveys the impression of his capacity to be at ease and serene in spite of these problems.

KRENG CHAI: This freedom of action implied by a "cool heart" seems to be a paradox to one of the more important points of the Thai value system - KRENG CHAI - respect for superiors with humility and obedience to authority. The KRENG CHAI trait goes along with the Buddhist thought of "Right Speech" as it tends to discourage criticism while also working against social mobility. The operation of this concept is so strong that middlemen are used to negotiate between socially distanced individuals on different strata. Social distance is not to be violated so that often inconsequential speech is substituted for emotionally loaded and potentially dangerous interchange. Often this small talk is utilized as the guardian against giving social offense while the Thai explore the situation and make a decision to withdraw as gracefully as possible or if the conditions are right, to continue with the more serious matter undergirding the encounter.

Interestingly enough, the Thai cultural freedom of action and individuality are so highly prized and so much a fact of life, that the Thai seems to shape his military environment rather than to be shaped by it. Thus the Thai military encounters cultural situations

74

unknown to most American Commands. One of these problems is a result of the Buddhist precept "Refrain from taking life". The Thai is not emasculated by his religious beliefs to the degree that he will not fight, but due to pressures of belief and societal forces, he goes about his combat in a manner quite different than do the Americans. He avoids conflict situations as much as possible and tends to engage in battle only when other alternatives are denied. In theory, only defensive military operations can be tolerated.

Due to these concepts of taking life, "Search and Destroy" operations, by conscious or unconscious design, often seem to degenerate into noisy search and little destruction. This approach permits each serviceman or combat unit to adopt the attitude that any life taken will be done by someone else. It also permits a skillful enemy to demonstrate "staying power", etc. to degrees beyond reasonable expectations.

It has been observed that indirect fire weapons have been aimed at innocuous parcels of ground, usually out of sight of the gunner. The observer doesn't fire the weapon, and the gunner does not decide when to fire the weapon. The consequences of the projectile are not fully registered to any single individual ..... Taking life is a most serious offense to the Thai Buddhist and must not be lightly brushed away or scoffed at as a primary factor influencing behavior... killing just isn't done if it can at all be avoided. For example, execution of criminals, when they are scheduled, is nearly always the job of a non-Buddhist executioner. [15]

15. Thomas C. Wyatt, (Unpublished manuscript) "Impact of Certain Social Psychological Factors on Royal Thai Army Counterinsurgency Military Operations", February 1968, Chapter III (No pagination)

These cultural values sometimes tend to permit military units not to aggressively seek out the enemy. It also permits failure to rapidly close with him in mortal combat. Even when these two events have happened and the enemy is decisively beaten and attempts to withdraw, swift pursuit does not seem too popular.

The Thai quality of KRENG CHAI prevents, or at least hinders, individual initative within the service as it pressures each man to stay within his own level and not to assume authority or privileges of a higher social or military level. Thus, instead of instantly acting as events and conditions may warrant, the cultural inclination is to stop and wait for orders from a higher level. Likewise, the concept of the illusionary nature of matter and depreciation of material possessions create problems of adequate preventative maintenance for machinery and rolling-stock. There is a considerable difference of attitudes by the Thai and the Americans in this respect so that the replacement costs of equipment is proportionally higher for the Thai. [16]

---

16. These observations are based upon repeated on-site visits within Thailand 1966-1968; on interviews with Thai officials, foreign advisors, missionaries and foreign cultural students within the country.

PROBLEM SOLVING: Work patterns and habits are developed over a period of years with each individual reflecting both the characteristics of his society, his personal experiences and propsensities. Generally around the world, Americans have acquired a reputation of setting and following a fast and continuing work pace which is frequently criticized by others. A desire to attain greater professional skill, technical proficiency, "to get on with the job", to improve oneself, and enjoy the benefits thereof, are characteristics which the Americans like to attribute to themselves. These are qualities which the American society admires and rewards.

One could well describe the American approach to most problems as impersonal and technical. However, in Thailand the emphasis is more aimed at the manipulation of personal relationships than upon the execution of sheer professional competence. What may appear to achievement-oriented impersonal scientific societies as adequate motivation for self-improvement, in Thailand's personally oriented society may be outweighed by many other factors.

Work patterns and solutions may be evidenced also by the way men approach a task - by negative or positive attitudes toward work achievement. To many Americans "A problem identified is a problem half-solved". The logic system of the American is generally geared to a sequential and pragmatic approach to problem solving. Particularly is this true where the American self-image is concerned. This is the way many solve their problems where it be the technical task of developing systems engineering, developing ever larger computers or repairing a child's doll.

In Thailand, however, identification of a problem is by no means any indication that a feasible solution will be quickly nor easily formulated and executed, or for that matter, even be seriously considered as requiring action. Here, things are sometimes done differently or left undone completely. Unless this fact of life is recognized and realistically accepted, frustrations tend to overwhelm the non-Thai.

When carefully drawn plans are upset, when losses instead of gains occur, some Thai seem to think that Dukkha is more the cause than inefficiency. Moreover, Thai culture encourages the idea that successes or failures are the result of karmic law than they are of present skillful or unskillful actions. The present and future - immediate or long range - is controlled by the actor whether in this existence, previous ones or those yet to come. Life's total course is programmed by each individual rather than a superior power so that dukkha is always controlled by karmic law.

Equanimity is the only way to face such an existence according to the Thai. Equanimity is the practiced habit of a peaceful mind able to repell anything which disturbs it. While dukkha is a "sense of continuous misery", equanimity prevents the individual becoming overly disturbed by it. The Thai have a descriptive phrase for this which is heard very frequently, "MAI PEN RAI!", "It doesn't matter"! "MAI PEN RAI as a facade, may be interpreted as Thai politeness, as an apathetic response, as lethargic license, fatalism or as an acceptance of the incident as Karmic so that a sense of equanimity is the only viable solution. It is such a basic part of the fabric of Thai politeness utilized for the reduction of interpersonal stress, that foreigners may have problems knowing just what real meaning it may convey.

Within the context of problem-solving, it is also appropriate to mention the Buddhist idea of Right Speech. Often a new manager or a new military commander may hesitate to create drastic changes of organization of methods of operation as these may be interpreted as adverse criticism of one's predecessor. This concept also may create difficult circumstances due to the idea that criticism is wrong. Thus solutions to problems may be made difficult as even objective observations may be interpreted as blame. If fault is found with an established system, it will reflect unfavorably on one's supervisors and the operators of the system. So it is considered best to remain quiet and make do with less than an adequate operation.

Since one must avoid discredit to others, even unfilled requisitions for essential items must not be questioned. Pushing, persistent inquiries by the requester is considered to harm others so that demerit falls on the one creating the request. This concept results in the thought that the unprocessed requisitions are the responsibility of those in authority of requisition operations rather than the originator of the request. Within the military this attitude may result in the "dead-lining" of vital equipment or the inability to effectively execute assigned missions. In other occupations the results may be just as harmful although not immediately apparent.

Another factor that may have strong influences on problem-solving is the Buddhist idea that existence is prolonged through desire or craving. Since the cultural pattern is to refrain from these thoughts, it is wrong to seek for sensual pleasures, material gains or acquirement of less tangible but equally accepted authority, power, fame, popularity, etc. Thus, to be hard working, ambitious and energetic invites the prolonging of samsara and additional reincarnations. Therefore inactivity may be due to laziness, lethargy, apathy, indifference, climatic conditions, diet, disease or a

valid belief in the currently taught ethical teaching of the Buddha.
Some Thai declare that the ones who demonstrate an acquisitive
drive illustrate a conflict phenomenon between Buddhist doctrines and
natural inclinations. Wealth, influence, positions of power, etc, are
then explained as the results of actions in one's previous existences
which have created these favorable conditions for the individual as
just rewards.

SOCIAL PATTERNS: One of the most important rules of Thai
social bahavior is to maintain smooth interpersonal relations. While
the rural Thai may seem to worry "more about their stomachs than their
hearts", [17] Phillips declares that this may be "expressions of an
existential anxiety about the essential instability, uncertainty, and
impermanence of all life (including their own), an anxiety which has
its cognitive basis in the 'Wheel of Law' and other Buddhist doctrine". [18]
They tend to avoid overt expressions of hostility and open conflict by
withdrawing rather than have aggressive encounters. Were uninhibit-

---

17. Phillips, op. cit. p. 201

18. Ibid, p. 202

ed aggression permitted, a fundamentally distasteful degree of involvement in each other's lives would result.

The almost profound sense of self-concern with personal freedom-of-choice appears to encourage the rural Thai to ignore or emotionally isolate himself from the influence and effects of others to a remarkable degree. Withdrawal may be interpreted as the use of isolation due to difficulties of relating to others, or more likely to the rural Thai being emotionally tough with sufficient self reliance and emotional security that the need of others is not imperative. [19]

Generally the connections between religious or ethical values and behavior patterns are not articulated. These connections are interwoven in the cultural millieu so that conscious perception is seldomly evident. There is one definitive pattern pertaining to the concept of individuality that accounts for much of the foci of life. This is the assumption that much of the individual's basic character is born with him with many of his tendencies already well formed due to previous existences. This belief not only affects childhood,

---

19. Confer Phillips, p. 206

but the whole life as it is built around the concept that each individual is so uniquely different in his way to Nibbana that otherside interference is wrong. It is evident in the way that Thai businessmen complain about their workers being so unreliable; in workers who absent themselves from their jobs without warning or excuse; in employees who simply walk off the job and don't come back or even leave word of their departure.

CHARITY: Typical Buddhist practices in Thailand have traditionally been "materialistic" in the sense they have supported the peoples' concerns at a static level not too much above subsistence. Charity has not therefore been so freely distributed in Thailand as in some Western countries. This is in full accord with the Thai concept of the Karmic Law however. Belief in this doctrine declares that an unsatisfactory status is the result of one's previous non-merit actions. Why should one be relieved of punishment? If it is avoided now, which it most likely cannot, it will only come later in stronger form because of its delay. This law of cause and result is a significant behavioral control factor in Thailand. Yet, it is not fully complied with as the Thai have many hospitals, dispensaries and other agencies to aid the distressed.

EXPEDIENCY: Kingshill in his study of a village in Northern

Thailand declares that a trait of the villagers is expediency and the willingness to do something if its value is apparent, provided it will not be boring or require excessive amounts of energy. [20] It is possible to see that possible tensions between the practices essential to modernity, newly introduced into Thailand, with the traditional short-term expediency and freedom from annoyance which accompanies the Thai value of expediency. It is still difficult to find in Thai culture the overwhelming urge to dominate, master and use nature that is an essential attitude for industrial development in the west.

KWAM SANUG: Kwam sanug has a very high value throughout Thailand. This refers to a sense of pleasure or happiness that must be present in either leisure or work. Even a task that may be profitable may be dropped if it does not prove to be enjoyable or fun. Many of the rural people seem to think that unless activity

---

20. Konrad Kingshill, KUDAENG - The Red Tomb, pp. 7. Incidently, athough some social scientists do not like Kingshill's book, the only valid argument they use when pressed for its errors is that it oversimplifies and thereby may distort an accurate evaluation. Simplification always creates generalities that may require clarification, but are not necessarily incorrect.

has the potential of fun it is not worth doing.[21]   Phillips says "... sanug
seems to reflect an attempt on the part of the villagers to lead a psy-
chologically intergrated life, wherein time and energy one gives to an
activity is rewarded immediately and directly with pleasure."[22]
Undoubtedly this concept will create tensions when confronted with the
essential efficiency of modernity. This will surely occur as sanug is
an unforced, uncalculated spontaneous theme which planned use of
resources, time and efficiency will challenge.

Happiness seems to be the apex and sum of the other Thai qualities,
values and behaviorisms. It is descriptive of the uncomplusive enjoyment of life which is the ideal of the Thai. It is in agreement with
Buddhist teachings in the sense that most people are still far from
Nibbana so that when happiness is achieved, one's Kamma must not be
too bad. But life is not ideal and tensions do appear to be unavoidable
in many instances. When these confront the individual and alternatives
have negative value to him, he may simply escape the situation by

---

21. Kingshill, pp. 8-9 , Phillips, p. 61; Bruce Morgan, Thai
Buddhism and American Protestantism, Chiengmai, Thailand, Thailand
Theological Seminary, 1966, p. 78; Robert L. Mole, 1968 Field-notes.

22. Phillips, p. 60

leaving without a word. Thus many homes are broken up, families scattered, and the community seems to accept it as natural with the karmic law undergirding the whole fabric.

Sometimes when the situation becomes too tense, one may brood behind socially acceptable devices for a time. The time span will depend upon the degree of involvement. Then internal pressures may result in direct or indirect socially acceptable behavior. This may be the verbalization or acting out of displeasure against an inanimate object or an animal owned by, and within the perceptual distance of his superior. In some cases, the individual may be moved to sudden and violent action such as killing those deemed responsible for the problem. A scrutiny of Bangkok newspapers for one month disclosed numerous crimes of passion indicative of strong suppressed emotions exploding into sudden violence. Realization that repressed emotions may erupt in violence may be an important factor in the reluctance of employers to directly "fire" or dismiss employees. It does help to account for the indirect method of expressing displeasure or means of imposing one's desire over another. It helps to explain what appears to many foreigners as an extraordinary veneer of politeness that makes Thailand "the land of smiles".

DAILY LIFE: The teachings of Buddhism are absorbed from earliest childhood as a nautral part of the environment. Within school, many precepts are recited until they become second nature even though many schools are no longer under control of the Sangha or located on the wats or even taught by monks. Moreover, a very high per centage of rural males spend at least a three months period as monks which reinforces both concepts and behavior patterns. In most areas, marriage arrangements with parents are very difficult unless the male has been a monk for a period of time. Social pressure produces conformity in most instances.[23]

Monks are not allowed to refuse any food offered to them. Buddhist etiquette requires the monk not to speak or show signs of any emotion toward those who earn merit by sharing food or other offerings. No thanks are given by the monk. Rather, the gift of food to the monks confers a blessing, "merit", on the giver so that the monk is to be thanked for giving opportunity for merit to the householder or any member of the laity. If more than one monk goes to a community for merit offerings of a morning, etiquette requires them to come and go in single file without conversation with anyone. Thai monks are

---

23. William J. Klausner, Popular Buddhism in Northeast Thailand, paper prepared for the Wenner-Gren Foundation for Anthropological Research, 1962 Summer Symposium; also Klausner's lecture at the East-West Center in Bangkok, 1965; Mole, 1968 Field-notes.

required to spend each night during the formally declared Period of Rain in their own monasteries. At other times, with permission of the abbot, they may stay overnight at other monasteries. When offering homage to the Buddha, represented by his image, Thai Buddhists generally light three incense sticks and a candle besides placing a lotus blossom or other flower in front of the statue.

In the Thai tradition, invitations to one's home are reserved for the most intimate friends or immediate family. Financial strain in returning a foreigner's hospitality may preclude acceptance to eat in a foreigner's home. This is not normally expressed, but results in the Thai simply not appearing at the appointed time. This is acceptable among the Thai and is thought to be a graceful solution to a difficult situation.

It is customary to remove one's shoes upon entering a Thai home. This is not practiced in public places except for the temples where it is mandatory. The wearing of one's shoes in a Thai home is interpreted as an expression superiority to one's host.

The Thai always attempt to quickly ascertain one's status and rank within the social system. This is essential so that speech and mannerisms can be adjusted accordingly. To raise one's voice, especially toward a superior or one's elders, is considered very impolite. To shout or scream at another person is always thought to be in bad taste and revealing a definite lack of CHAI YEN. Even a demonstration of impatience is thought to result from an inadequate understanding of the problems involved, or more acceptable ways of getting a task completed. Likewise to look some-one straight in the face is thought to be both improper and rude. Instead, the Thai are taught when in close proximity to someone to avert the face and eyes slightly so that observation is done through the corner of one's vision. This is in contrast to the cultural custom of America where interest, attention and respect are shown by looking directly at the face of another. [25]

Social status is always of concern when two or more Thai are in association with each other. Generally, an informal atmosphere or discussion is preferred by the Thai as this permits the side-stepping of an issue without the necessity of a firm commitment even when dealing with foreigners. To facilitate such encounters the Thai give

---

25. This writer was present when a Thai speaking American boy in Chiengmai was scolded by an adult Thai for looking directly at the King and Queen as they passed by in an automobile on a formal occasion. When this was explained as an American custom showing respect and honor, the Thai walked away wondering about these strange customs. The formal occasion incidently was the acceptance of the second white elephant born during this present reign with the ceremony in early 1966. This particular elephant died in the Spring of 1968.

the appearance of being easy-going, care-free and owners of a delightful sense of humor. However, such manifestations of affability, apparent gaiety, etc., may not be a reflection of carefree lightheartedness, but techniques in which inconsequential, jovial, entertaining facades prevent the necessity of serious or unpleasent decisions. Generally, tne only way to establish effective intimacy is through a superior-subordinate, patron-client relationship.

The Thai have few or no dietary taboos even though the Sangha does. Respect for living things do not prevent the Thai from the use of flesh foods even though some rural Thai claim that they don't kill fish. They simply put them on the bank, and if the fish dies, it would be wrong to let it be a waste. Although the Buddha is reputed to have discouraged the use of alcohol as a drink, many Thai do use it for this purpose. Moreover, a rather strong beer is manufactured, sold and consumed within Thailand. The daily papers show pictures of the elite at cocktail parties, and many rural stores carry some type of alcoholic drink as a standard item.

The uncertainties of a "highly fluid society" create the need for players in this social climate to continuously be alert. The social hierarchy must be scanned up and down to confirm and hold one's place. Thus, a stranger needs to be introduced by a known individual to receive acceptance, and benefits are reserved for one's own superiors or subordinates as the case may be. While looking up and down the social strata, one must not forget to make side glances as someone out there may be a potential rival for a higher position. If there is, he will be given no quarter nor will he ask for any for it would be in vain.

The impermanence of such arrangements soon wilts the Westerner who has no immunity to the seemingly chaos which continues. In the ever shifting Thai scene, promises and contracts sincerely made are only feeble indicators of future intentions which may change without warning or notice. Even though Buddhism provides a moral and ethical system, each individual is free to make his own interpretations as self-reliance is a fundamental Thai value. Emphasis on the individuality of each person within the Kamma encourages social mobility and changing positions once one has moved beyond the basic level of existence. Some times a Thai may seek to reduce uncertainity by wearing a miniature image of the Buddha (Phra) around his neck, or may use amulets, tatoo marks or other devices as contributors to success.

PHRA PHUM: No study of Thai value-behavior relationships could omit some discussion of Phra Phum and claim any validity as it is present everywhere. Phra Phum is the shrine of the guardian

91

spirit found in the compounds, yards, hotel roofs, etc, throughout Thailand. Normally mounted on a post, the small house built in temple-form may contain a small statue, incense, food, flowers, elephants, figures of dancing girls or other symbols of gratitude to the guardian spirit. When a Thai is invited to stay overnight in a home, it is customary to pay respects to the hosts' Phra Phum and ask permission to stay. Then prior to leaving, one is supposed to again pay respects to the guardian spirit, thank it for its hospitality and ask for a safe journey. The home owner who starts out with a small house usually has a small spirit house also. As prosperity becomes evident by the ownership of a car, a T.V. set, etc, and as better living conditions are possible, the spirit house will be improved or replaced with a larger and nicer one.

If one of the family has a premonition of misfortune, wants to receive special help, or has a need for the impossible to happen, the spirit is approached in a respectful manner with burning incense and a lighted candle. To encourage a favorable response, the spirit may be promised a cocoanut, chicken or duck. In some cases a number of servants, elephants or horses may be offered instead. Then if the request is granted and the rewards are not given to the spirit, evil will happen to the one who made the promise or nightmares will prevent him sleeping. Thus, the miniature servants of clay and paper animals which appear in the little houses symbolize answered prayers. Besides the Phra Phum, there are nine other household spirits with one of them dwelling in the threshold Thus when one passes throught the doorway, proper procedure is to step over the threshold rather than on it.

One group of Thai citizens not previously discussed here are the Muslims of South Thailand. They have intense religious and cultural feelings which sets them apart from the ethnic Thai to a greater degree than the ethnic Chinese or any other of the larger minority groups within the country. Normally the Muslims identify themselves more with Malay cultures than with that of Thailand proper. Generally, the Muslim area is a sophisticated society with traditions comparable in age and elaboration with that of the Buddhist. Both the Muslim and Buddhist communities are theocratic in concept to a very large degree. The interweaving of secular and religious duties is so close in Thailand that it would be very difficult for a Muslim to ever become a national figure with political power and fame.

Very little research of a scientific nature has been done insofar as Thai Muslim values and behavior patterns inter-relate to those of the Thai Buddhists. This is now being attempted by Dr. Jacques Amyot of

Chulalongkorn University, who, with a large number of graduate studies, is intensively studying beliefs, values, behavior patterns, etc., of a successful Muslim community in central Thailand. The findings of this extended study will be of significant value as it studies Muslim, ethnic Thai and others who are in the area and the relationships between the various peoples in their interactions. Until initial papers of this study are presented, it would be unwise to guess their findings. However, the success of the Thai government in placing Buddhist settlers in predominant Muslim areas as a means of building national identity has yet to be proven. A short term view would indicate that such moves create tensions rather than provide a genuine help. But if one thinks in terms of an endless cycle, it is possible that the net effect will be a valid endeavor.

Thailand's geographic divisions definitely influence values as the Thai pragmatically adjust to the situations where they find themselves. While the underlying values are much the same throughout the nation, except in the extreme Muslim South, economic factors modify practical utilization of these. For instance, in Northeast Thailand nationalism is much more important currently than it is in the central section of the country.

In this geographic area of insurgency, nationalism has several facets. Economic development is foremost due to the nature of the area and the difficulty of earning a living. The young people of the area, who have the greatest exposure to urban life, feel that it is a national responsibility to improve the economic conditions of the area. Due to the low standards of living, many Northeasterners feel the government considers them to be second class citizens. The insurgents utilize this theme in their propaganda efforts against the central government also. Thus, some of the Northeasterners feel that they have to prove that they are 100% Thai. The drive toward this goal increases their desire to preserve the "Thai way of life". This is especially noted in the localities where some of the poorer features of Western culture are prominent. These cities are generally near the military bases currently utilized by American military personnel. The northeasterner has strong feelings about the Vietnamese and Chinese in the area also. These emotions include resentment, hostility, envy, and some fear due to the Vietnamese and Chinese business acumen that often results in monopolies for these ethnic groups.

The Northeasterner's strong emotional attachment to kinship groups and villages promote problems of cultural adjustment. Consequently most of them prefer to remain in the area, and when they do migrate, they generally settle in communities composed of other Northeasterners.

95

The value systems of the Northeasterner come from local (superstitions) animism, Buddhism and the socio-economic factors of life. The Buddhist concept of a good leader is <u>Prom Viharn Sii,</u> "benevolent, just and upright". The King is seen by a number of the rural Thai as such a person with real goodness, kindness, just, upright and concerned about his peoples' needs. Many tend to identify with the Thai monarch in almost a spiritual sense for they see him as the embodiment of certain divinity or at the very least, one who has earned very much merit in prvious existences. Therefore for some of the rural Northeasterners, the King and Queen are symbols of worship even more than they are symbols of the nation.

Many of these Thai appear to think that the primary aims of nationalism ought to be the preservation of the King, the Buddha and national independence. Nevertheless, their primary loyalty is more to kinfolk and good friends than to the nation. The goverment is often viewed as almost a supernatural power utterly beyond their influence or control, so why be concerned with it. Agents of the insurgency attempt to convince the local folk that the government is really a "devil" or it would have done much more for them. Unless both security and economic hopes are realized to a greater extent, the insurgents may grow much stronger and gradually develop a firmer base of operations.

The Northeasterner seems to have only a minor interest in free speech, press, assembly, etc. They much more desire to live in peace with freedom to work their land as they please, with freedom of religion and the right to practice village customs. Attitudes toward foreigners vary according to the circumstances of encounter and the density of foreigners and the frequency of cross-cultural contacts. [26]

Detailed discussions about the inter-relationships of Thai values and behavior could continue indefinitely. However much of it would be a mere expansion or repetition of values and behaviorisms already brought to view. Therefore the following chapter is an attempt to draw valid conclusions of the inter-relationships of Thai values and practices with awareness of possible effects of modernization now in progress in Thailand.

---

26. Confer Klausner, op. cit; David E. Pfanner and Jasper Ingersoll, "Theravada Buddhism and Village Economic Behavior" JOURNAL OF ASIAN STUDIES (21) 1962, pp. 341-361

27. Confer Appendices A-E for numerous details and guidelines for developing insights into Thai values based upon their practices or that which they desire of foreigners. Also confer with Manning Nash, Editor, Anthropological Studies in Theravada Buddhism, Cultural Report Series No 13, Southeast Asia Studies, Yale University, 1966; Howard Keva Kaufman, Bangkhuad, Locust Valley, New York, J. J. Augustin Incorporated 1960; Current research under the direction of Dr. Somchai Rakwijit, Ph. D. in Northeast Thailand offers the hope of being one of the most exhaustive studies of Thai value and behavior patterns for the foreseeable future.

CHAPTER V

MODERNIZATION EFFECTS ON THAI VALUE-BEHAVIOR PATTERNS

> By oneself is evil done;
> By oneself one suffers;
> By oneself evil is left undone;
> By oneself one is purified. [1]

Religion exceeds the multitudes of rituals and beliefs in its base as a culture process in man's inner self. More than mere sets of distinct rules and laws which guide men in their lives, hopes and behaviorisms, religion is a product of countless generations. Through the centuries it has progressed with slow development through infinitesimal cultural processes having infinite purposes and leaving traceable influences. Religion conveys man's painful never ending search for the powers that determine both temporary and permanent destinies. According to many authorities, as man has groped his way through time, he has constantly

---

1. Dhamapada, English version by Dr. Luang Suriabongs, Buddhism In Thailand, Bangkok, Prae Bhittaya Ltd., 1954, p. 20

modified, revised and reoriented his concepts of this mysterious destiny-determining power. [2] This has seemed essential for better, easier and more meaningful ways of coexisting with this supernatural force with some sense of harmony and meaningfulness of existence.

Differences in culture often make great differences in the ways by which various peoples solve their problems and develop attitudes affecting every phase of life. What seems completely normal, natural and proper in one society may appear utterly ridiculous in another. A basic undergirding of any society's reactions to serious challenges for development of socio-economic standards is its Weltanschauung, world view, as determined by religeo-ethical concepts.

The Thai Weltanschauung was by and large represented by Theravada Buddhism. It emphasized the primacy of personal values and thus fortified individualism. Few commitments or obligations for the furtherance of social goals were expected or provided for. While one's status was determined by achievement rather than through ascriptive norms, it was the manipulation of other human beings rather than creativity which counted . Choei and sanuk militated against the extreme commitment and the sustained hard (and often unpleasant) work required for the establishment and operation of modern industrial undertakings. The Thai value highly those who are quick to take advantage of opportunities when these present themselves, but seldom would they take the trouble to create such

---

2. Confer Fred L. Parrish, A History of Religion, New York: Pageant Press, 1965; Edward Norbeck, Religion In Primitive Society, New York, Harper and Row, 1961.

opportunities, or cooperate with others in such an endeavor.
The role of merit-making as a kind of investment reduced the
incentive for economically productive investments. As for
political motivation to action, the Thai feeling of loyalty to the
Government . . . was more of the nature of passive obedience
than of active loyalty. [3]

Ayal continued his indictment of the Thai cultural pattern

regarding economic development by noting the non-existence of a

multiplicity of Buddhist sects. He declared this is significant as it

indicates an absence of intellectual restlessness. [4] His observation

may or may not be true since other factors appear to be ignored.

The non-existence of numerous sects may be an indication that the

State has tight control of the Sangha. It may also infer sufficient

freedom of theological thought within the Sangha that organizational

conflicts and reform are not deemed essential. It could indicate

the philosophy that all is illusionary, and even be an excellent

example of individual non-involvement which is an ideal of Budanism.

Individual involvement, concern and commitment are essential for

any new organizational growth, development and sustenance. Also

---

3. Eliezar B. Ayal, "Value Systems and Economic Development
In Japan and Thailand", THE JOURNAL OF SOCIAL ISSUES, January
1963, Vol. XIX, No. 1, (pp. 44-51) p. 50

4. Ibid,

it may be that Ayal is correct!

It is true that within Thailand, Buddhism is a symbol of conserva-
tion and unity. Yet healthy religions demonstrate remarkable resiliency
and power for regeneration when confronted with serious challenges.
Buddhism, having survived this long, most likely will not cease to
exist or fail to influence Thai values and behavior. When major cultural
and social changes occur within a society several things may happen to
its religious bases. Sometimes the religions may die as they did in
Greece and Rome; they may be replaced by pseudo-religions that
nominally retain the basic religious core; the status religion may lose
its position to a "new religion" that sweeps the country; or it may
creatively respond to the challenges and mold them into acceptable
patterns. Even when the latter is true, dramatic social changes create
secularization to varying degrees.

One of the basic problems confronting the Thai is how to best meet
and handle the secularization which accompanies industrialization,
modernization and scientific education required for the twentieth
century. The current aggressive attempts to meet these challenges
create the probability that the culture and personality of the nation will
still be characteristically flavered by Buddhist thought and practices.
The forces of education, international trade, military considerations,

political pressures, developing entrepreneurship, etc., may become strong enough to overwhelm Buddhist influences on the processes of change momentarily. But should this occur, it would not necessarily ordain the death of Buddhism. More likely it would tend to become an anchor to which the Thai could cling for refuge while everything else undergoes the violent stresses of rapid social change.

Winston King, while analyzing the forces of change throughout Buddhist Asia, wrote of the future in terms that applies to Thailand in so far as its core values and practices are concerned. Although sympathetically stated, his observations are of value to anyone seeking to understand how changes may be accepted, rejected, modified or otherwise treated. Certainly it has value to those involved in the current Thai-American partnership.

> ... it is unlikely unless it turns to a crass, rootless
> materialism that the Buddhist East will abandon its will-
> to-detachment or its negatively-stated but affirmatively
> lived ideal of individualism. It will undoubtedly continue
> to be sceptical of an absolute, fanatical devotion to the
> improvement of samsara (the social-political-economic
> conditions of the space-time order) as anything but
> frustrating and exhausting in the long run ... It may
> translate detachment into "disinterested" i.e. unselfish,
> public concern and service. It may achieve a new pattern
> of relaxed, moment-by-moment attention to matters in
> hand, be they this-world or other-wordly, and thereby
> avoid many of the soul-destroying inner tensions of West-
> ern society. It may evolve a dispassionate but not apathetic

102

and a balanced but not static, mode of action which will
provide a clear-headed unemotional, but not indifferent
solution of political and social problems.

The widespread modern practice of meditation . . .
represents a significant contemporary effort to achieve
such balance. But whether this will in fact take place
and whether Buddhism will be able basically to formulate
its own terms for such an actionable positive-negative
synthesis of values, is by no means certain. The pace
of change may be so rapid that a Western-style positivism
will be forced upon it whether or no. [5]

All meaningful discussions of modernization processes in
Thailand must include awareness that a least 80 per cent of the
population is engaged in agricultural pursuits. [6] Even after a
hundred years of the commercial revolution, subsistence is still
the basis of rural household economy. Nevertheless, the stability
and security of rural life in Thailand are conditions which are
essential to the makeup of the nation's present and social economic
situation. These underlie and make possible certain characteristics
of the contemporary government. Consiquently the urgency for
rapid industrialization, mass education and consumer goods have
not here-to-fore been a major concern to anyone outside of a very
small educated minority. A survey of economics in 1957 allowed

5. Winston King, A Thousand Lives Away, (1964) p. 40.

6. George M. Kahin, (editor) Government and Politics of Southeast Asia, Ithaca, New York, Cornell University Press, 1964, p. 31

the report to say, "A peculiar difficulty in the case of Thailand is that not only is there no systematic plan for economic development but there is no very intense demand or desire for economic development."[7] This observation has now been changed inasmuch as Thailand is presently in its second National Plan. This national planning has come into being due to the ruling elite determining that it would be good for the nation. These long range plans are not the result of any pressures created by the mass consumer. In any case, the effective development of such plans will create conflicts with the traditional ideals of Buddhism.

Having never undergone Western colonial rule, Thailand has a social structure which admirably illustrates its utilization of the Western economic system. Its agricultural taxation, its banking and trade patterns, its methods of industrialization all have unique features. Generally, these have evolved due to the Thai capacity to learn by experience while using the aid of foreigners without allowing them to dominate the cultural fabric. The Thai have always attempted to maintain a freedom to manoeuvre in relations with other nations, and seem to feel a definite uneasiness when this is not possible. Even while circumstances may require temporary reliance on one particular

---

7. Thailand, Economic Survey Group, Report on Economic Development Plans, Bangkok, 1957, mimeographed, p. 11, quoted by Kahin, op. cit., p. 61

power, the Thai carefully develop counter balances as rapidly as possible. Even now while joined in a military alliance with the United States, Thailand seeks to attract aid, techniques and investment from other countries. Also it strives for utilization of regional organizations and elements of the United Nations which may serve as counter balances to United States pressures. [8]

In this process, the Thai are introducing techniques and institutions developed in social systems based upon functional specialization and rationally derived practices of the West. These are being brought into the distinctly different Thai social pattern to fulfill Thai purposes. As this practice continues, the apparent conflict between Buddhism and materialistic development creates ambivalence and a sense of disquiet is some sincere Thai businessmen. One of the basic Buddhist values is the enjoyment of a non-complusive life. This conflicts with the value of economic development having rapid growth whose fruits lead to ever-rising standards of material well-being. However, leading members of the Sangha and the Department of Religious Affairs are aware of the problem and are determined to deal with such issues in distinctly Buddhist ways. The success of their

---

8. Confer T. H. Silcock, Editor, Thailand: Social and Economic Studies in Development, Canberra, Australian National University Press, 1967, pp. 20-26.

goals will do much to determine the future cultural patterns of the nations. But even the answers being formulated must depend to a very large degree upon how well the United States maintains its economic-political-military posture in Southeast Asia. [9]

Economic development is normally accompanied by a sense of restless aggressive acquisitiveness in the population at large. An illustration of this is the multi-billion dollar advertising industry which is dedicated to creating awareness of, and desirability for, new products and stimulating appropriate actions for the acquirement of the advertised product. In pursuit of customers for the particular product, advertisers play upon man's natural desires. This is in contrast to Buddhism which stresses that such desires are to be repressed and subdued as these prolong samsara. The Middle Way's whole thrust appears to be in opposition to materialistic acquirement.

Nevertheless, consumer urgency is a dynamic and vital factor in economic growth. Only as the levels of consumption rise can manfacturers expand their companies with all the implication which such development possesses. Generally, the Westerner's materialism is considered to be amoral so long as immoral means of

---

9. Kahin, op. cit., p. 67

acquiring its benefits are not involved. Buddhism's teachings have not been interpreted in a similar nature however. The desire to gain benefits making life more pleasant does not have the blessing of the Buddha's dogma always. In spite of Buddhistic non-approval, the current generation of Thai college students desire many of the same goals that American students do, and as they assume roles of influence, secularization will surely increase. Their desires, and those of others influenced by similar factors, can promote development toward a more modernized nation. This is clearly recognized by the Royal Government which desires the benefits of the twentieth century, but wants these fitted into a cultural mold formulated through many centuries.

Until the present time, the desired changes have been introduced into Thailand by the small number of elite who constitute a three-tiered pyramid. At the very top of the pyramid is the King. Many Thai consider that all authority and power is derived from the King. This concept is closely related to the King's position as a Buddharaja. The basic concept of Buddharaja appears to have come from the Hindu-Mahayana background of Cambodia. This belief has long been indigenized into Thai culture and Buddhist practices. Incidently, in a similar manner, the Brahmins in the royal palace have been

Buddhized. There seems to be no conscious conflict in the Brahmin roles with those of the Sangha in royal ceremonies even when these involve the installation of the Thai kings on their thrones.

Technically, immediately below the King is the Prime Minister. He, with some ten to fifteen persons, forms the top layer of the pyramid. These are the real rulers of the central government since the King is a constitutional monarch. [10] Immediately below them is perhaps a thousand people forming the second layer of the pyramid as key members of the ruling elite. The third layer of the pyramid is the educated and articulate political public who serve to execute the policies determined by the top layer. The whole ruling class of Thailand does not constitute more than two per cent of the adult population. Yet Hanks and Philips say that "group coherence depends on status inequality", [12] They also argue that "it is difficult for an equal to give anything of

10. The present constitution, signed by His Royal Majesty King Bhumibol Adulyadej on Thursday 20 June 1968, is the eighth constitution in the 36 years of "constitutional government" since the 1932 coup.

11. L.M. Hanks and Herbert P. Phillips, "A Young Thai From the Countryside", in B. Kaplan (Editor), Studying Personality Cross Culturally, 1961 quoted in David A. Wilson's, Politics in Thailand, 1962, p.181.

108

value to an equal or command his respect". [12.]

Class distinctions are arbitrary, but still a fact of particular importance for understanding Thai society and that social movement appears relatively easy. The criteria for class status are - money, family, education, type of work and general way of life - and it is not difficult to move up or down the scale. Yet, Thai society is very status conscious and the concept of equalitarianism is virtually incomprehensible to the Thai if Kamma is not consciously considered and accepted. In it, high status is a sign of good kamma and meritorious worth. If someone in a high position loses his status, it is thought that his kamma has been used up and he has not sufficiently replenished it to counter-balance bad kamma from the past. After all, religion ordains that a man's fate is a matter of his responsibility, and his position is a matter of his personal relationships with other individuals. [13] Still this same religious force makes the Thai of all classes resist regimentation, systematization and routine of all types.

While the rural peasant continues his time honored practices, the Thai elite know that progress may demand changes in their social

_____

12. Ibid

13. Kahin, op. cit., p. 41

109

customs and political structures. They also realize these changes require analysis, training and sustained effort which may not always agree with popular thought. Innovations must originate at the top in Thailand due to its pyramid structure and undergirding values. Royal patronage of moderization activities have generally encouraged many Thai to expect and accept changes in social patterns and economic activities. The government has been pragmatic enough to learn through its mistakes without ideology preventing essential changes. Instead the close coordination of the government and the Sangha permit cooperation in the promotion of approved programs.

CONCLUSIONS: It seems evident that Phillips and Kingshill are basically correct in their generalizations of basic Thai values. Although their terms appear over-simplistic, no scientific data yet invalidates their analyses. Economic, geographic and education factors may modify and reconstruct their order of values, but do not refute the findings of these and other cultural scientists. Sociological studies evaluating values and behaviorism with their similarities and differences due to economic, political, social and geographical factors are currently in process. However, it will be some months before their findings are released as acceptable scientific data. Like Guskin's study, these will determine priority

of values and the significance of each in relation to current conditions
in Thailand. These studies contain potential values for the Thai
government for planning purposes, and for the American allies in
association with Thai citizens.

> It is evident that in Buddhism the Thai intellectual has
> a Weltanchauung which is both satisfactory and comfortable.
> This faith in traditional religion has saved him from heart-
> rending introspection and self-criticism and has preserved
> for him a matter of fact approach to life. The Thai intel-
> lectual is above all pragmatic rather than speculative . . .
> Most educated Thai are officials faced daily with stubborn
> facts of life. They are not therefore given to flights of
> imagination. They fit comfortably into an established struc-
> ture of organization. They are not stimulated by idleness
> and failure to an examination of the fundamentals of that
> structure or the ultimate upon which it is based. [14]

A Thai psychologist, trained in the West, in discussing the

traits of his people, has noted a number of characteristics as descriptive

of his countrymen.

> . . . the Thai in general were hospitable people; that
> the tempo of their lives was slow; that they possessed con-
> siderable equanimity; that many Thai actions had a basis
> in the Buddhist religion; that the Thai respected age; that
> the Thai, although capable of making rapid cultural
> adaptations at least on a superficial level, were basically
> conservative; that ritual and ceremony were important
> parts of Thai life; that the Thai were not steadfast; that
> they were extravagant; that they were bashful, introverted;

---

14. David A. Wilson, "Thailand and Marxism", in Frank N. Trager's
edition of, Marxism in Southeast Asia, Stanford, California. Standford
University Press, 1959, pp. 59-60 and 67.

that they were not socially minded, that is, they were
not joiners; that the Thai approach to life's concerns
were empirical rather than theoretical; that the Thai
were indolent; that they were egoistic, self-centered;
that they lack persistence, "stick-to-it-iveness" and
that the Thai were a mild people, a non-violent people.[15]

On-site research tends to confirm much of the foregoing,

and the preceeding chapters have attempted to explain the dynamics

involved. Thai "bashfulness" is more a reflection of Thai culture

than of true introvertism. The Thai must not upset his superior-

subordinate relationships to secure essential or greatly desired

items. This does not seem to hinder the expectation or request

that Americans secure such materials for him. Repeated inquiry

as to why this procedure is acceptable resulted in answers

summerized in the following terms:

> Buddhism is for Buddhists. Its teachings are for its
> adherents with little expectation that non-adherents will
> follow its guidance. Moreover, the non-Buddhist may do
> things which adherents ought not to do. Thus, the
> American, generally being non-Buddhist, are exempt
> from factors controlling Thai Buddhist behavior. There-
> fore it is not wrong to ask you to help secure the items
> in a manner which would be inconsistent with Thai ideals.[16]

---

15. Lauriston Sharp, Frank J. Moore, Walter F. Vella and
associates, Thailand, New Haven, Conn., Human Relations Area
Files, Inc., 1956, p.231.

16. Robert L. Mole, 1968 Field-notes on Thailand.

This study, along with the authorities quoted there in, demonstrates an obvious vital inter-relationship between Thai values based on Buddhism and Thai behavior patterns in general. The close cooperation and administration of the Sangha by the government, and its use in developing nationalism necessiates awareness of Buddhist values.

Modernization and current international pressures on and in Thailand raises questions requiring futher research, These questions include: (1) What adjustments of values are necessary for the development of a valid vital sense of nationalism so that insurgency cannot develop an effective base within the country; (2) can Buddhist dogma be effectively reinterpreted so that belief systems and modernization trends harmonize rather than conflict? (3) How can the predominant Buddhist Thai values be effectively blended with those of the Muslims and the tribespeople so that these minorities can be accepted as equal participants in the Kingdom; (4) what major American and Thai values can be interchanged for valid contributions to each other's culture, and how could these be effected; (5) are there any of the Thai values which may be introduced and shared with other developing Southeast Asian countires? Surely a people who have survived so long, and whc have a unique culture, have qualities worth the serious attention of those priviledged to linger a time in the "land of smiles".

BIBLIOGRAPHY

BIBLIOGRAPHY

Arensberg, Conrad and Arthur H. Niehoff, Introducing Social Change, Chicago, Aldine Publishing Company, 1964

Ayal, Eliezer B., "Value Systems and Economic Development in Japan and Thailand", JOURNAL OF SOCIAL ISSUES, January 1963, Vol. XIX, No. I

BANGKOK WORLD, 9 May 1968, Special Report: Evaluation of Thailand's Economic Development - Development of Education.

Basham, A. L., The Wonder That Was India, New York, Grove Press, Inc., 1954.

Beny, Ernst, Buddhism or Communism, Which Holds the Future of Asia, Garden City, New York, Doubleday and Company, 1965.

Cady, John F., Southeast Asia: Its Historical Development, New York, McGraw-Hill, 1964.

Chakrabongse, Prince Chula, "Buddhism in Thailand", Vistas of Thailand, Bangkok, Government Public Relations Department, 1963.

Coedes, George, The Making of Southeast Asia, translated by H. M. Wright, Berkeley, University of California Press, 1966.

Coomaraswamy, Ananda, K.. Buddha and the Gospel of Buddhism, New York, Harper Torchbooks, 1916.

Dhaninivat, Prince H. H., Monarchical Protection of the Buddhist Church in Siam, Bangkok, World Fellowship of Buddhists, 1964.

Eliot, Sir Charles, Hinduism and Buddhism, A Historical Sketch, Vol. III, London, Routledge and Kegan Paul, 1857.

Embree, John F., "Thailand - A Loosely-structured Social System," AMERICAN ANTHROPOLOGIST, 52:181-193, (1950).

Gard, Richard, Buddhism, New York Braziller Press, 1962.

Goldsen, Rose, K.M. Rosenberg, R.M. Williams, Jr., E.A. Suchman, What College Students Think, Princeton; M.J.D Van Nostrand, Co.; 1960.

Guskin, Alan E., Changing Values of Thai College Students, Bangkok, Chulalongkorn University, 1964

Harvey, G.E., History of Burma, London, Longmans, Green and Company, 1925.

Hastings, James, Editor, Encyclopaedia of Religion and Ethics, New York, Charles Scribner's Sons, 1910.

Heine, Goldern, Robert, Concept of State and Kingship in Southeast Asia, Ithica, Cornell University Press, 1956

Humphreys, Christmas, Buddhism, Baltimore, Md. Penquin Books, 1951

Huq, Muhammad Shamsul, Education and Development Strategy in South and Southeast Asia, Honolulu, East-West Press, 1965

Kaplan, B., Editor, Studying Personality Cross Culturally, Evanston, Ill. Row, Peterson and Company, 1961.

Kaufman, Howard Keva, Bangkhuad, A Community Study in Thailand, Locust Valley, New York, J.J. Augustin Incorporated, 1960.

Kahin, George, McTurnan, Editor, Government and Politics of Southeast Asia, Ithaca, New York, Cornell University Press, 1964.

Kingshill, Konard, Kudaeng, The Red Tomb, Bangkok, Bangkok Christian College, 1965.

Klausner, William J., Popular Buddhism in Northeast Thailand, Bangkok, Wenner-Gren Foundation For Anthropological Research, 1962.

Kluckhohn, Clyde, Mirror For Man, Greenwich, Conn, Fawcett Premier Book, 1965

Koch, Sigmund, Editor, Psychology: A Study of a Science, New York, McGraw Hill, 1959.

Landon, Kenneth P., Southeast Asia: Crossroads of Religion, Chicago, University of Chicago Press, 1949.

Learner, Daniel and Wilbur Schram, Communication and Change in the Developing Countries, Honolulu, East-West Center Press, 1967.

Luang, B.B., The History of Buddhism in Thailand, Bangkok, Chatra Press, 1955.

Mole, Robert L., The Role of Buddhism in the Contemporary Development of Thailand, COMNAVSUPPACT SAIGON FPO 96626, Navy Personal Response, 1968.

Mole, Robert L., Vietnamese Time Concepts and Behavior Patterns, Saigon, South Vietnam, Navy Personal Response, 1968.

Morgan, Bruce, Thai Buddhism and American Protestantism, Chiengmai Thailand, Thailand Theological Seminary, 1966.

Morgan, Kenneth, The Path of the Buddha; Buddhism Interpreted by Buddhists, New York, Ronald Press, 1956.

Nakamura, Hajime, Ways of Thinking of Eastern Peoples, Honolulu, East-West Center Press, 1964.

Nash, Manning, Anthropolgical Studies in Theavada Buddhism, Southeast Asian Studies, Yale University, 1966.

Nida, Eugence A. and William Smalley, Introducing Animism, New York Friendship Press, 1959.

Norbeck, Edward, Religion in Primitive Society, New York, Harper and Row, 1961.

Opler, M.E., "Themes as Dynamic Forces in Culture", AMERICAN JOURNAL OF SOCIOLOGY, November 1945, (51:3)

Parrish, Fred L., A History of Religion, New York, Pageant Press, 1965

Phillips, Herbert, Thai Peasant Psychology, Berkeley and Los Angeles, University of California Press, 1966

Prabha, C. Buddhist Holy Days and State Ceremonies of Thailand, Bangkok, Prae Pittaka Publishing Company, 1964

Sharp, Lauriston, Frank J. Moore, Waller F. Vells et al, Thailand, New Haven, Conn.

Silcock, T.H. (Editor) Thailand Social and Economic Studies In Development. Canberra, Australian University Press, 1967

Sinder Leon, "A Brief Sketch of Hinayana Buddhism In Thailand", JOURNAL OF ASIAN STUDIES. Vol. 7, No. I P. 1964

Suriabongs, Luang, Buddhism In Thailand, Bangkok, Prae Bhittays Ltd. 1954

Thailand Official Yearbook 1964, Bangkok, Government Printing Office,

Thompson, Virginia, Thailand, The New Siam, New York.

Trager, Frank M., Editor, Marxism In South East Asia, Stanford, Col. Stanford University Press, 1959

Wales, H.G.Q., Siamese State Ceremonies, Their History and Function, London, B. Quaritch, 1931

Wales, H.G.Q., Ancient Siamese Government and Administration, London, B. Quaritch 1934.

Wells, Kenneth W. Thai Buddhism, Its Rites and Rituals, Bangkok, The Christian Book Stone, 1960.

Welty, Thomas, The Asians, Their Heritage and Their Destiny, Philadelphia, J.B. Lippincott Company, 1963.

Wilson, David, Politics In Thailand, Ithaca, Cornell University Press, 1963

Wood, W.A.R. History of Thailand, London, Fisher, Uwin, 1926.

Wright, Michael A. "Some Observations on Thai Animism" PRACTICAL
    ANTHROPOLOGY, Jan-Feb. 1968

Zaehner, Robert Charles, The Concise Encyclopoedia of Living
    Religions, New York, Hawthorn Books, Inc. 1959

UNPUBLISHED MANUSCRIPT

An additional source of information has been the excellent unpublished
manuscript "Impact of Certain Social Psychological Factors on Royal
Thai Army Counterinsurgency Military Operations" by Thomas C.
Wyatt. This paper written in 1968 is by an American scholar who is
also, or has been, an ordained monk of the Thai Sangha. Because
Mr. Wyatt apparently intends to prepare this matter for inclusion
in a proposed book, sincere appreciation is expressed to him for
a couple of short quotations which have been properly footnoted.

Additional field-notes gathered from throughout Thailand and other
areas of Southeast Asia form the basis of statements and opinions not
formally credited to some other source.

APPENDIX A

WHAT NEEDS TO BE KNOWN ABOUT THAI MANNERS AND CUSTOMS

Commander Robert L. Mole, Chaplain, United States Navy was assigned in the summer of 1965 the task of instituting an effective cross-cultural program within the Navy/Marine environment. This project was under the sponsorship of the Commanding General, Fleet Marine Force, Pacific, and the Chief of Chaplains, United States Navy. This assignment envisioned both library studies and on-site research with subsequent preparation of information for all Navy/Marine personnel assigned to Southeast Asia.

In the winter of 1965-6, research was conducted in Thailand for a number of weeks. Among those who were briefed on the objectives and methods of Chaplain Mole's mission was Colonel Pin Mutukan, Director General, Department of Religious Affairs, Ministry of Education, Royal Government of Thailand. Colonel Pin demonstrated his interest in the cross-cultural study by encouraging that informal requests be made to the Chief of Chaplains, Royal Thai Army, for assistance. Courtesy calls were made and assistance of the Chief of Chaplains was graciously provided. The basic question to be answered by the Chaplains of the Royal Thai Army was, "What should Americans know about Thai manners and customs in order to avoid offense and to establish friendship predicated upon understanding?" The following is a translation of the Thai document received from the Chief of Chaplains office through the cooperation and interest of Colonel Pin.

WHAT NEEDS TO BE KNOWN ABOUT THAI MANNERS AND CUSTOMS

1. What the Thai people respect most and are very sensitive about:

The King, Thailand's Chief of State, and the Queen are most respected and therefore disparaging comments should be avoided.

Buddhism is Thailand's national religion. Buddhist monks form a special group located above politics and are to be respected like members of any other religions.

Pagodas, religious images, Buddha's bones, temples, religious shrines or any other religious places draw special respect from the Thai people.

The Thai people have high respect for their parents; elder members of their family, teachers and professors for the very important part they have played in their life.

The high respect extended to parents and elder members of the family lead the Thai people to respect their ancestors, and such respect is shown to statues, pictures, images and monuments representing these ancestors.

2. How respect is expressed:

The Thai people greet one another by bringing the palms of their hands together, fingers extended and joined, in front of their face (the Wai gesture). Men accompany this gesture with the oral expression of Sawasdi, Khrap to both sexes and women say Sawadi, Kha to both sexes.

Shaking hands is not yet widely practiced by the majority of the Thai people, especially the rural people. Furthermore, it is not appropriate for a man and wife to embrace and kiss in public.

The "Wai" gesture, when addressed to an elder person, is done by bringing the thumbs at nose level, and lowering the head a bit. Bringing the hands too high is not appropriate in this case.

In expressing respect in religious shrines or to monks, one must kneel, and three times, make the "Wai" gesture, and after each time, bend the head all the way down in front of the knees with the hands in the same position until they reach the floor, where they are then placed down to bring the palms of the hands on the floor, thumbs touching each other, then bring the head up again to the "Wai" gesture.

In paying respect to religious images, one does the same as to religious shrines and to monks. One must however be careful not to place religious images in low places or in inappropriate places such as among bottles of liquor. Religious images are not to be used as articles of decoration, or for instance using them as hat or coat hangers.

Since Buddhist monks form a highly respected group, one must behave and act accordingly. Some suggestions could be made here:

a. When a monk is visiting, one should stand up and accompany him in and out.

b. When walking, avoid obstructing the way of the monk.

c. One should offer one's seat to monks in public transportation.

d. One should not sit higher than a monk, nor stand close or sit pressed against him, and above all one must not touch his head.

e. One should not shake hands or greet a monk in a familiar way that one would greet a friend.

Offering things to monks is considered to be a gesture of sincere respect and has nothing whatsoever to do with alms-giving to beggars for instance. What is given to wats is used for the benefit of the people in general, such as building shrines to permit the faithful to worship. Even military units make voluntary contributions in support of the Buddhist religion.

When going to worship in religious shrines, one usually takes along flowers, joss sticks and candles, or in some cases, thin sheets of gold to be adhered to Buddha statues.

When standing before an elderly, respected person, or for that matter, anything respected, Thai people stand erect, with arms down along the sides, and above all without putting the hands in the pockets. When greater respect is to be shown, one bends forward, head down a bit, and hands on top of each other at buckle level.

When sitting, in the same circumstances as described above, one sits in a folded-leg position (to avoid lengthy description please refer to the posture of the "Mermaid of Copenhagen"). When greater respect is to be shown, as for instance to monks, elderly persons, one puts the elbows down touching the floor near the knees while keeping the "Mermaid" position, making the "Wai" gesture with hands and head down to almost touching the floor. And whenever one finds oneself in the "Mermaid" sitting position and one speaks to or is spoken to by the person to whom one is showing respect, one holds the "Mermaid" position, head up and hands at the "Wai" position. If one finds oneself sitting in a chair, one should not cross one's legs, for such a posture would be disrespectful.

3. It is not the custom of the Thai people to keep their shoes on while walking in the house. One should therefore be mindful to take off one's shoes before entering a Thai home. Such a custom however, is not followed in public places, in offices and stores for instance.

Shoes must also be taken off when entering the home of monks, or when stepping into altar rooms of temples.

Shoes must be taken off when stepping into a boat which serves as both shop and home of the merchants. Furthermore, one should avoid stepping on the bow of the boat for such an action would do offense to the "Goddess of the Trade" and bring bad luck. Exceptions to this rule are boats for hire, taxi-boats and ocean going craft.

4. Habits concerning hats and umbrellas

Upon entering temples or any other places of worship, hats should be taken off and umbrellas lowered, for not doing so would be a sign of disrespect.

5. Practices in the Thai government service (civil and military)

It is customary in the government service, especially in the military, to show respect according to rank. When talking to a superior or a higher ranking officer, one does not stand or sit on a higher level, one does not sit with his legs crossed, one does not stand with hands in pockets.

It is considered impolite by Thai people to sit and extend one's legs on the table or on the sides of an armchair.

When a superior steps up to the desk of a lower ranking official to address the latter, the latter must stand up to speak with his superior until he is told to sit down or until the superior leaves.

6. Touching someone else's head is not practiced in Thai society

If one is not well acquainted with another person as one would be with a very close friend, one should avoid tapping or touching the other person's head, even in a friendly way. There are of course some exceptions to this rule, as for instance an adult could tap the head of a child in a parent-like manner.

Hats are also considered to be something that one should take particular care of. They should be hung high enough to avoid being stepped over. On the contrary, shoes are considered to be something one looks down upon, and therefore are not to be placed in high places. It is also considered very impolite to use one's foot to point.

7. In one's daily social contact with the Thai people, one should take note of a few points. Like many other people, the Thais have their own characteristics:

They like to be free and dislike to look down on other people
They are not agressive by nature
They are generally generous
They like to look upon others as friends
They are generally of a happy nature

Because of all these characteristics and because Thailand has never been under foreign rule, the Thai people tend to look upon strangers as friends. They do not carry out their daily life with an overwhelming obsession for money nor in an excessively intent fashion.

Thai rural people, especially in the North and the Northeast, usually wave a friendly hand when passing somebody, even if the latter is a complete stranger to them. This is a sign of their good intentions and friendliness.

In rural areas, lacking hotel facilities, travellers needing accommodation can usually freely rest in temples after contacting the head monk of the temple. He can also seek accommodation in the house of the village chief, of the district chief, or of any local inhabitant for it is customary for the rural people to offer to travellers.

In Thai practice, the "Dutch Treat" or "American Share" system is not followed when going out in a group. It is customary for the oldest person of the group or the one financially better off to pay for everybody. However, someone else in the group sometimes offers to cover the expenses in order to help the oldest person.

The "Tip" system, although practiced, is not followed in all cases. When one hires somebody and prices have been agreed upon, it is not customary to give extra money.

If one insists however, in giving somebody something, one should offer gifts in the form of merchandise, for such an action has a better sentimental value and is the expression of one's friendship and gratitude.

Upon receiving presents and gifts, the Thai people do not usually open them at once for such an action could be interpreted as being needy. They therefore prefer to wait for more privacy.

Thai rural people like **casualness and** friendliness. They would therefore be pleased if their guests would put aside all formalities and talk and behave in a casual and friendly manner.

It is customary for local inhabitants in rural areas to offer cold water and cigarettes to their guests, and if it is meal time, whatever food is available at the time. The Thai people like to eat with fork and spoon but such utensils are sometimes lacking in some parts of rural areas and some local folk still have to eat with their hands, although such a practice is more and more fought against by the government on grounds of health.

The Thai people usually say "Mai Pen Rai" (Never Mind) as an expression of instant forgiveness. In answer to a "Thanks", the Thai people may also say "Mai Ren Rai" which in this instance would mean "Don't Mention It".

8. Advice as to how to behave toward the opposite sex;

It need not be mentioned here, that universal gentleman's behavior toward women applies in Thailand as well as anywhere else. The advice given in paragraph two should be kept in mind in this case. However, one should know that in Thailand, the husband is the head of the household.

9. Some Thai customs that should be known;

At a marriage, it is customary for Thai people to extend invitations for the lustral water pouring ceremony. Upon receiving the lustral water, one pays respect to the Buddha image by bowing and then proceeds to pour the water on the hands of the bride and the groom, no matter in what order, and at the same time, makes wishes of happiness to the couple.

It is customary for young male Buddhists to be initiated into monkhood when they reach the age of twenty. Such an initiation takes about three months and is aimed at training young men into reaching spiritual maturity. Guests are usually invited to attend the ceremony held at the temple of the young man's family's choosing, and would in this case bring gifts which would usually consist of things of everyday utility.

The Thai people hold rituals for the dead. People newly deceased are bathed before being placed into the coffin. In rural areas, such a ceremony is held by the dead person's relatives themselves. In town, and if the deceased is well known and respected, it is customary to invite guests to the ceremony and the latter consists of pouring specially prepared water on the hands of the dead person.

It is also customary in Thailand to cremate the dead rather than bury them. In some rural areas, it is not necessary to issue invitations to attend the ceremony for in small communities people are well acquainted and are willing to give a helping hand in making all the preparations. In town or some other areas, invitations are issued. The ceremony is rather simple and of short duration. Candles, flowers and joss-sticks are issued and one proceeds toward the coffin, bow or wai in sign of respect, place the objects in front of the coffin, bow or wai once more, this ends paying respect. The ceremony is then over, and before departing, one may sometimes receive booklets which briefly relate the life of the deceased.

Important Buddhist dates are observed by government officials and military units as official holidays and if the foreigner participates in the various ceremonies it would strengthen friendship. Some of these important Buddhist occasions are, just to cite a few:

a. The Makhabucha, which falls in the middle of February (3rd) lunar month), is the date at which time Buddha assembled His disciples to teach them the fundamental principles of the Buddhist religion.

b. The Visaghabucha, which falls in the middle of May, is the date of celebrating birth, death, and enlightenment of Buddha.

c. The Asarahabucha, which falls in the middle of July, at which date Buddha first began teaching his disciples .

The Thai people have festivity seasons which, for civic action sake, should be followed whenever possible:

a. The Songkhran Season - This is the Thai New Year which falls between April 13 to 17, and at which time people present food to monks, bathe their Buddha images and express their respect to their elders. It is also a custom at this time of the year to throw water at one another in a spirit of good humor and friendship.

b. The New year Season - This falls on the 1st of January, at which date, the people present food to monks and pay their respect to their elders.

c. The Buddhist Lent Season - This falls on the 1st waning moon of the month of July, at which date monks hold religious ceremonies and the people present them with candles to be used by the monks during the three-month period when they are confined to stay in the temples every night.

d. The Thod Kathin Season - This falls between the 1st waning moon in October and the middle of November. The Thai Buddhists must present yellow robes and other gifts to the monks. On this occasion money is presented for repairs to be undertaken in the different wats. All military units participate in such ceremonies and offerings.

AND MOST IMPORTANT OF ALL:

One must remember that when one goes to Thailand as a friend and is mindful to respect its customs and traditions, one is always welcomed by the Thai people.

****

APPENDIX B

THE THAI COUNSEL FOREIGNERS

In February, 1966 CDR Robert L. Mole, CHC, USN, Navy Personal Response, made a courtesy call to Major General (Air Marshall) MANOB AVM SURIYA, Commanding General, Military Research and Development Center, Ministry of Defense, Royal Thai Government. The Air Marshall expressed appreciation of American efforts to build teamwork, partnership and rapport on a "two-way street" understanding. In cooperation with the objectives of Personal Response, he therefore immediately prepared a memorandum for his office staff. He asked that they list items which they believed Americans ought to know in order to avoid needless proplems in Thailand. The original answers of the 51 participants in Thai are given here. This is a listing of answers without editing or condensing, as even repetition reveals multiplied concern to some extent. The translations are by Thai employees of USOM in Thailand.

APPENDIX B

THE THAI COUNSEL FOREIGNERS

1. Thais do not believe in:
   A. Using Buddha images in decoration and display.
   B. Displaying signs of affection (kissing and fondling) in public places
   C. Placing feet upon desks and tables.

2. It is not considered seemly to:
   A. Adopt ungainly or obnoxious postures when in the presence of an elder or superior.
   B. Use images of the Lord Buddha or portions thereof for purposes of decoration.
   C. Elevate the feet to a prominent level during a seated conversation.
   D. Crossing of the leg while seated with an older person or a superior.
   E. Take the lead while walking with an older person or a superior.

3. A. It is not polite to use the foot for pointing.
   B. The phrase "Faithful dog" should not be used as an analogy.
   C. The duties of the off-spring are to provide for the care and welfare of the parents to show gratefulness.
   D. Buddhist monks are not beggars and are not parasites of society.

4. A. If a person carries Buddha images on his person he should not walk under cloth-lines; enter into brothels or in any manner place the images in a "low" place.
   B. Proper reverence and respect should be paid to Buddhist priests at every opportunity (even though that priest before being ordained may be your son or your servant.
   C. Food alms should be properly given to the receiving hand of the priest. In the case of a women giver, an article must be placed on the cloth of the priest which he holds.

5. A. Proper respect must be paid to elders (superior).

6. A. Shoes should be removed while entering places of worship.
   B. Priests are considered to be representatives of The Lord Buddha and one should not act in a familiar manner with them.
   C. The Buddhists revere their priests, proper respect should be paid to them.

7. A. When entering Buddhist temple or shrines remove shoes, hats and pay proper repect as one would do to any place of worship.
   B. Show proper respect to priests and representation or representative of the religion.
   C. Refrain from making comments desultory or insulting to the religion.
   D. When discussing religion with those who are knowledgeable of the subject, logic and reason must be employed. The religion allows for intelligent discussion or criticism.
   E. The feet are not considered the proper appendage with which to point.
   F. Refrain from touching the arm, hand, or other familiarity when greeting a Thai woman.

8. A. Refrain in from making criticisms of the ceremonies of the Buddhist religion. (taking of alms of the priests)
   B. Buddha images or parts thereof should not be used for decorative purposes.

9. A. Kindliness, gentleness and generosity are qualities of the good Buddhist.
   B. If it is understood that Thais (Buddhists) expect the same courtesy towards their religion as Americans expect to be expended to their religion, all will be well.

10. A. It is not in Thai tradition to hug, kiss or otherwise show signs of familiarity to women in public.
    B. It is not in Thai tradition to greet or congratulate a woman by kissing (wedding etc.)

11. A. Avoid condescending attitudes or gestures.
    B. Genuine friendliness is appreciated by Thais or Americans, Buddhists or Christians.
    C. Things, objects of reverence or respect should not be utilized other than the purpose for which it was intended.

12. A. Thais consider the foot "low"; it should not be used in pointing.
    B. For solemn occasions and functions the colors to wear should be somber colors or white.
    C. Buddha images should not be utilized as utensils or decorations.

13. A. Do not elevate the foot it is considered low.
    B. "High" things such as hats, books, flags should not be placed where they can be stepped upon.
    C. Buddha images should not be placed or utilized as utensils or decoration.

14. A. A mutual respect should be paid to respective religions.
    B. Must mutually keep the faith.
    C. Forgiveness for errors.

15. Buddhists do not:
    A. Covet thy neighbors wife or children.
    B. Openly and in public display signs of affection.
    C. Be of an insulting or condescending attitude.

16. A. Allow respect to the aged, aid and abet children and women at every opportunity.
    B. Show proper respect to places and articles of worship.
    C. Kindliness and gentility are the most important Buddhist qualities.

17. A. Legs should not be crossed while seated in temple.
    B. Derogatory comments should not be made about Thailand or about the Thai people being uncivilized.

18. A. Hats and shoes should be removed before entering temple.
    B. Obnoxious noises and sounds (conversation) should be avoided during ceremony.
    C. Temple is the place for meditation.

19. A. Shoes should be removed in entering a Thai home.
    B. Public display of affection must be avoided.
    C. The "Wai" is the accepted method of greeting among the Thais not the handshake.

20. A. Thais do not like public display of affection (kissing and hugging)
    B. Feet are considered "low" and must not be used in pointing.
    C. Buddha images are objects of reverence and should not be used for other purposes.

21. A. When conversing with priest, it is improper to sit crosslegged.
    B. It is forbidden to place Buddha images other than in proper shrines.
    C. It is proper to remove hat and shoes when entering place of worship.

22. A. The Thai greeting is to "wai".
    B. It is improper to touch the person of a Thai lady in greeting (other familiarity).

23. A. Buddha images are not to be used in decoration.

24. A. Images of The Lord Buddha or parts should not be utilized for decorative purposes.
    B. Public display of affection between the sexes is considered improper.
    C. Politeness is an important prerequisite in any Thai relationship (particularly with an elder).

25. A. Kindliness and gentility are important desirable Thai qualities.
    B. Buddhists show proper respect and reverence to persons and objects and shrines of their religion.
    C. The touching of another person before having received consent of that person is frowned upon.

26. A. Religion should be mutally respected.
    B. Hats should be removed while entering a temple.
    C. Shoes should be removed while entering a temple.

27. A. Buddhists respect and revere their elders.
    B. Grown-ups should not browbeat children.
    C. The reality of life process of the Buddhist is: growth, age (illness), death, birth.

28. A. In conversing with elders it is polite to show proper respect and interest.
    B. The function of the hand i. e. pointing, handling and passing objects should be done with the hand. It is impolite to point with the feet.
    C. Objects of reverence (Buddha images) should not be utilized in decorative schemes or as utensils.

29. A. Mutual respect should be paid to places and objects of worship according to tradition.
    B. Work should be done through proper allocated channels.
    C. Mutual respect and co-operation in common projects.

30. A. Thais do not display signs of affection in public.
    B. It is considered highly improper to commit familiarities with the opposite sex (the touching of hands and arms).
    C. Politeness and courtesy should be observed during conversation.

31. A. The Buddhist is respectful towards places of worship, monks and images of Buddha.
    B. Greeting is done by the "wai".
    C. Buddhist believe in and practice alms giving.

32. A. It is not proper to place the feet on the desk.
    B. It is impolite not to show proper respect for your elders and superiors.

33. A. The purchasing and selling of images of Buddha and parts and portion of images is considered improper conduct.
    B. Proper respect should be payed when entering a place of worship.
    C. It is considered disrespectful to stand and sit at a level which is higher than shrines.

34. A. Thai people do not like loud sounds, loud or other generally obnoxious behavior.
    B. It is considered by Thais traditionally that the head is a "high" object, and not to be trifled with.
    C. Places of worship of the religion should be shown proper respect: i.e. the removal of shoes and hat before entering same.

35. A. Hats should not be worn into temples and wats.
    B. Buddha images should not be placed in inappropriate places.
    C. Giving alms to the monks is considered traditional and accepted practice.

36. A. Show proper respect to elders and superiors.
    B. Have proper respect for your fellow man.
    C. Help aid and assist the weaker sex and children in any way you can.

37. A. Out-siders should not go to places of worship unless they have proper attitudes.
    B. It is considered proper in Thailand to pay respect to ones elders and superiors.
    C. It is improper to show physical signs of affection in public places.

38. A. The threshold beam (a beam of any material) at the entrance of a temple should be stepped over and not stepped on.
    B. It is not considered proper to sit in a cross-legged attitude when in conversation with monks.
    C. Kindliness is an important virtue that all people should strive to achieve.

39. A. The feet are considered "low" appendages and should not be elevated to places of prominence.
    B. It is not considered proper to use terms of endearment such as "darling", "honey" to an excess.
    C. Proper respect should be paid to monks when attending Thai ceremonies.

40. A. It is desirable that Christians acquire some knowledge of Buddhist ways and traditions. Misunderstanding often arises from the insufficiency of knowledge of one another's customs and traditions.

41. A. To establish a good easy relationship between one another based on understanding.
    B. Lies and falsity, insults and condescendation have no place in good relationship.

42. A. Skepticism and derogatory remarks made on another's person or on people's religion should be avoided.
    B. Politeness should be observed at all times in dealing with senior or elderly peoples.
    C. Courtesies should be extended towards women and elders.

43. A. Covetness of "thy neighbors" should be avoided.
    B. Respect and courtesies should be paid to women and elders.
    C. Overt signs of affection, physically touching a person of the opposite sex in public should be avoided.

44. A. Impoliteness should be avoided in any relationship with a senior or elder person.
    B. It is right and proper that proper respect should be paid to places of worship and reverence of another religion.
    C. Hats and shoes should not be worn into the temple of the wat.

45. A. Thais do not generally appreciate insulting and derogatory gestures and comments.
    B. Buddha images are objects of worship and should not be utilized in schemes of decoration and/or as utensils.

46. A. Proper respect should be payed to places and persons of the Buddhist religion.
    B. The feet are not the appendages with which to point.
    C. Proper respect should be used in speech with senior or older persons.

47. A. Proper respect should be payed to shrines and other places of worship of our religion.
    B. Proper respect should be payed to senior or older persons.

48. A. Thais should revere the Buddhist Religion, the laws and the priests of the religion.
    B. Thais should pay close attention to the propieties.
    C. Cultural and traditional practices of the religion should be kept up and promoted.

49. A. Covetousness of the other person's property and family should be avoided.
    B. Thais respect their religion as well as seniors and elders.
    C. Proper respect should be paid to another man's religion regardless of one's personal beliefs.

50. A. Buddhists believe that kindliness is an important virtue.
    B. Buddhists pay appropriate respect to places of worship and represenatives of their religion.
    C. Buddha images should not be utilized in any way except in the ways for which they were intended.

51. A. Respect one another's religion.
    B. Keep faith with one another.
    C. Forgiving the trespasser or transgresser is a virtuous quality in the Buddhist religion.

APPENDIX C

HOW TO BE POLITE IN THAILAND

In 1957 Dr. Kenneth E. Wells, long-time missionary and learned
writer, wrote a short paper, "How To Be Polite In Thailand," which
apparently was never published in its final form. When interviewed
by CDR Robert L. Mole, Dr. Wells kindly gave him a copy of his
paper and authorized him to use it in the transcultural endeavor to
build understanding between the Thai and American people. With only
the omission of a sentence or two thought to be beyond the need of
the average American coming to Thailand, Dr. Wells' article is
produced here as it gives insights into behavior patterns based upon
Thai values. Dr. Wells was thanked at the time he gave this paper
to this reseacher, and he is again thanked for his kindness in sharing
a bit of his vast knowledge with others who need so desperately to
understand and appreciate peoples of cultures outside that of their own.

HOW TO BE POLITE IN THAILAND

As grandmother used to say,

> "Hearts, like doors, open with ease
>   to very tiny little keys;
> And two of these are
>   "Thank you" and "If you please."

The Thai are polite and they respond to politeness. The royal court set the pattern. The King, following a tradition going back to the Indian epics, is surrounded with an aura of divinity. It is held appropriate that His Majesty should be gracious to his subjects, and that they in turn should show respect, even reverence, toward him.

This concept of behavior appropriate to rank extends throughout Thai society, which is essentially non-egalitarian. A man has few equals; his own brothers, e.g., are either older or younger than he. It is fitting that precedence should be given to those of superior age, position, or birth. Right relationships, being on good terms with associates, contributes to an orderly society and to material success. An elderly servant may crouch before her young mistress, but the mistress addresses her by the honorific "Mae", "Mother".

The ingredients of good Thai manners are quiet speech, smiles, graciousness, and the utmost consideration for the comfort and "face" (dignity) of others.

A Bangkok visitor, glowing under a friendly welcome, will feel at home and deem Thai manners no different from his own. If he gets away from official receptions, however, and into small social groups predominantly Thai, he may suspect that his own rules of etiquette fall short of Thai standards. From the Thai point of view, loud chatter and quick hurried movements are associated with monkeys. In a classical dance, all motions are slow and graceful. Monarchs stride with the majesty of an elephant. The sage administrator is unruffled, never exhibiting loss of temper. Anger is immoral. The perfect lady is cool, trim, unassertive, yet gracious and quick to smile.

A westerner, about to appear on the social scene, might reflect that the Thai consider him potentially their social equal, but will assess his breeding, sincerity, and ability before taking him to their hearts. He should begin by exhibiting friendliness and quiet respect

137

toward those about him. He might observe that:

1. GREETING. Where hands are moist and sticky in tropical heat, warm handshakes lose their charm. Thai men, however, on being introduced, usually shake hands with a westerner as a concession to his custom. But the latter does not ingratiate himself with much handshaking. Often a bow, smile, and verbal greeting will suffice. In particular, westerners should not be zealous to grasp the hand or arm of a Thai lady, or to engage in hearty backslapping. Hands off is the best policy!

How do the Thai greet each other? They keep their distance, bow slightly and say "Swat-di" ("good fortune", swastika), bringing their hands, palms together, near or before the face. There is a touch of reverence in this. It is too formal to be repeated at frequent intervals. The one who is junior makes the first gesture; the senior must respond. In replying to a child he may, however, merely nod and say "Swat-di". Bringing the hands up (to wai) in respectful greeting contains social nuisa that may escape a foreigner. Rather than parody this fine gesture, the casual visitor should be hesitant about using it.

The expression "Swat-di" can also be used when parting from friends

2. DRESS. Clothes dignify the wearer and the occasion. Only cooli go shirtless. For men, white shirts with long sleeves, neckties, and coa are always good form, particularly when calling on officials or visiting temples and palaces. At formal dinners, white tuxedos and black trouser are in order. Gaudy shirts worn outside the trousers should be reserved for beach wear. Light-colored suits look cooler and better than dark one

For women, no hats, gloves, or stockings are necessary. Dresses should be conservative, not too decollete. Thai women consider black suitable only for funerals or deep mourning.

3. HOME DEPORTMENT. By long tradition, the person of greates dignity, e.g., a prince or an elderly Buddhist abbot, should sit on a leve higher than that of other persons present. In many social gatherings notl ing much can be done about this matter of elevation. But the observance should not be lost sight of, and a six foot Amazon can sometimes contrive sit low on a stool beside a venerated grandmother or grandfather and thus something to minimize her own height. Long ago she would have had to crouch on the floor.

Respect for a man's head is respect for the man himself. Brahman priests stress the sacredness of the top of the head. Animists once held that the top of the head was the abode of the kwan or spirit-self; and that the kwan was disturbed or alienated, the body sickened and died. There fore, if you accidentally touch a person's head, ask his pardon. A headsman would do the same to you before applying the axe. And do not pat children on the head to show approbation!

The lowly foot is held to be, figuratively as well as literally, the most debased part of the human anatomy, the area where insults are bred. Therefore keep your feet as much out of sight as possible. Do not sprawl or sit cross-legged with the sole of the foot toward the face of another person. Don't set your child up on a desk or counter with his feet pointing toward the heads of others. Don't use your foot to slide an object toward another person; don't point with your foot. You may point at distant objects with your finger, but never point your finger at a person. To point effectively, use your chin.

It is bad form to eat standing up or walking about. Cocktail parties do violence to this rule, but are tolerated as a necessary evil, particularly in diplomatic circles. But educated Thais would prefer to sit, eat slowly, and converse quietly.

In a home, it is not good form to handle Buddhist images or to ask questions about them unless the host takes the lead. The images are not simply examples of sculpture.

The exchange of small gifts as souvenirs of friendship is common practice. A gift or favor will invariably bring one in return. Gifts should be presented, or received, with the right hand.

4. WHAT TO SAY. A few don'ts: Don't be patronizing, critical, argumentative or bumptious. Don't begin sentences with "Why don't you. . . politics . . . canals . . . dogs . . . etc.?" Don't tell "How we do it". Don't ask personal questions. Avoid irony and difficult terminology because of language difficulties; English can be misunderstood. If you want an objective reply, don't ask leading questions. For example, "Why don't people like me?" would evoke assurances that you, above all others, possessed the utmost of popularity.

You can say "Kawp Koon", "Thank you", on numerous occasions, and "Kaw tote", "I beg your pardon", when appropriate.

5. TITLES AND MODES OF ADDRESS. To address the King or the nobility in Thai requires a complicated set of pronouns expressing "I" and "You" whereby each term reveals the five distinctions of the social status of the speaker and the one spoken too. A foreigner, fortunately, can resort to simpler European usage and terminology. One should say:

"Your Majesty" to the King or Queen.

"Your Royal Highness" to a child of a King.

"Your Highness" to a grandchild of a King, namely a Phra Ong Chao.

Some princes have the additional title of Kromamun, indicating high rank in government service, e.g., H.R.H. Kronamun Narathip Bongsprabandh (Prince Wan Waithayakorn, Minister of Foreign Affairs and (1947) President of the United Nations' General Assembly), and H.H. Kromamun Bidyalabh, (Prince Dhani Nivat, President of the Privy Council)

"Your Serene Highness" is the mode of address to a Mom Chao, i.e., the child of a Phra Ong Chao.

One can refer by name to the above members of the nobility as "Prince . . ." or "Princess . . .". A commoner who is wife of a Prince may prefer to be called "Princess . . ." although her correct title is "Mom". There are two ranks of nobility below that of Mom Chao: Mom Rajawong, child of a Mom Chao, addressed as "Mom Rajawong"; Mom Luang, child of a Mom Rajawong, addresses as "Mom Luang". The child of a Mom Luang is considered a commoner, and like all Thai, both men and women, can be introduced or addressed by the first name prefixed by the honorific "Khun".

A boy under fifteen is referred to as dek chai; a girl as dek ying. At the age of fifteen a boy becomes Nai (Mr.) and a girl becomes Nangsao: after marriage she is Nang (Mrs.). But in conversation, not Nai or Nang but "Khun . . ." (grace, excellence) is used when speaking of or to adults. Learned men, professors, are often addressed as "Achan." ("a" as in want). A child is commonly addressed as "Nu . . ." (rising tone).

In Thai circles it is correct form to approach the top man first in seeking a decision involving policy. Protocol, face, should never be lost sight of. Calling cards are useful in establishing personal contacts.

The words "Siam" and "Tical" are alien and somewhat archaic. "Thailand" and "baht" (rhymes with hot) are correct.

PRONUNCIATION:

The transliteration of Thai names into English presents difficulties. "Ph" is "p" (not "f"). Final "l" and "r" are pronounced "n". The name of His Majesty King Phumiphol Aduldet is pronounced "Poo-mee-pone Adoonlya-date". "Thai" is pronounced "Tai"; "th" is "t". "V" is pronounced "w"; "e" often has the force of long "a" as in "fate". Final "s" is pronounced "t". This seems unfair, but in Thai there is no final "s". "Theves", therefore, is pronounced "Tay-wait". The "a" as in "father" approximates the usual sound given to "a" in Thailand. In syllables such as "-arm", "-arn", and "orn". the "r" has no sound, but merely lengthens the preceding vowel, as in "Waithayadorn" . The Thai language has five tones, incomprehensible to the average tourist, but all-important in conveying thought.

A suggestion: A trip by taxi is cheaper if you ask the driver the fare before entering the cab. You will get along all right, and want to come back. Swat-di.

APPENDIX D

THE GREAT TRADITION OF THAI BUDDHISM

Awareness of Thai values and behavior patterns require a knowledge of the formal doctrines and authority of Buddhism. This very brief discussion provides a point of departure for those who require additional information. Undoubtedly it will prove sufficient for the largest percentage of Americans who read it in their role as allies of the Thai.

THE GREAT TRADITION OF THAI BUDDHISM

THE TIPITAKA "THREE BASKETS": THAI THERAVADA SCRIPTURES

It is believed that the First Buddhist Council met at Rajagaha within a few weeks after the Buddha's death, and among the items discussed, was that of the true Dhamma.[1] This council, supposedly, was composed of 500 Arhants, "holy men", dedicated to the seeking of Nibbana (Nirvana). Even though this Council met and determined the contents of the canon, the earliest ". . . direct evidence of the Tipitaka, as a whole, had already assumed its present form is furnished by the Milindapanha, which dates from the first century A.D."[2] Nevertheless, it is believed that the basic Pali canon was well fixed in the third century B.C.[3] While Buddhist scriptures are divided into four or five canons which range from those canonized soon after the Buddha's death to those formulated during the ninth to fourteenth centuries, the Pali canon is the one utilized in Thailand. It may be that adherency to a particular canon is largely determined by geography rather than such factors as historicity or logical persuasiveness.

Following the First Council after the demise of the Buddha, differences of opinion and personalities led to some eighteen sects or denominations within Theravada Buddhism.[4] One of these, the Vibhjjavadin is credited with the preparation of the Pali scriptures in the third century B.C.[5] "Pali is a literary form based on Magadhi, gradually developed, and perhaps only definitely fixed when the scriptures were first written down in Ceylon about 80 B.C."[6] Some scholars think that the actual writing may not have occured before 20 B.C,[7] yet the oldest of the contemporary documents of Buddhist literature, the Edicts of Asoka, inscribed on stone pillars, are written in a sister dialect called Kosala.[8]

1. B. Horner, "Buddhism: The Theravada", in The Concise Encyclopaedia of Living Religions, Robert Charles Zaehner, Editor, New York, Hawthorn Books, Inc. 1959, p.267

2. James Hastings, Editor, Encyclopaedia of Religion and Ethics, New York, Charles Scribners' Sons, 1910, Vol. VIII, p.86

3. Sir Charles Eliot, Hinduism and Buddhism, A Historical Sketch (3 Volumes) New York, Barnes and Noble, Inc. Reprint, 1962, Vol.I.291

4. Ananda K. Coomaraswamy, Buddha and the Gospel of Buddhism, New York, Harper Torchbooks, 1916, p.29: Edward Conze "Buddhism: The Mahayana" in R.C. Zaehner, A Concise Encyclopaedia of Living Faiths, p.296

5. Eliot, op. cit. p.276

6. Coomaraswamy, op. cit. p.259; Christmas Humphries, Buddhism, New York, Barnes and Noble, 1962, p.233

7. Ibid,

8. Coomaraswamy, p.259

For centuries the Tipitaka remained in the Pali version. It was written in Cambodian or Thai script on palm leaf strips with the words scratched into the surface and then inked with the rubbing of black powder. It has recently been translated into Thai. The Thai version has some 80 volumes, or one volume for each year of the Buddha's life.

The Pali canon utilized by the Thai consists of three major sections or "Baskets": (1) The Vinaya-Pitaka, "Rules of Discipline", for monks and nuns with regulations for monastic life (vinaya); (2) Sutta Pitaka, "Dhamma" or Basket of Discourses, composed of five collections of the Teachings believed to have been uttered by the Buddha; and (3) Abhidhamma-Pitaka which contains the psychological and philosophical terms of the Dhamma that are analysed, classified and expounded. [9]

The Vinaya-Pitaka, "Basket of Discipline", is basically the regulations for the management of the Sangha. It prescribes rules and regulations for the conduct of bhikkhus (monks) and bhikkhunies (nuns). It gives the rules for acceptance and reception into the Sangha, periodical confession of personal faults, conduct of life during the rainy season (roughly translated as Buddhist Lent), types of permissionable housing and clothing, various medical remedies and legal procedures for handling of schisms. While detailing the development of the Sangha, it also presents a rather full account of the life and ministry of the Buddha and relates a number of Buddha legends. [10]

This Basket of Discipline is divided into five books, which are: (1) Parajika "Major Offenses", which gives special cases and exceptions; (2) Pacittiya, "Minor Offenses", does the same for lesser offenses within the Order; (3) Mahavagga, "The Great Section", provides the rules for admission to the Sangha, procedures for ordination, clothing regulations, residence guide-lines, and the rules which govern special monastic activities and their performance; (4) Cullavagga, "Small Section", details the treatment, duties and offenses of teachers and novices, and the special rules for nuns; and (5) Parivara, Epitome of the Vinaya-Pitaka, which is basically a commentary on the Mahavagga, "Great Section", and relates legends and stories about the life of the Buddha following his Enlightement. [11]

---

9. Horner, op. cit. p. 268
10. Hastings, op. cit. Vol. VIII, p. 86; U. Thittila, "The Fundamental Principles of Theravada Buddhism" in K. W. Morgan, The Path of the Buddha, Buddhism Interpreted by Buddhists, New York, The Ronald Press Company, 1956, p. 68
11. U. Thittila, op. cit. p. 86; Hastings, op. cit. Vol. VIII, p. 86

The Sutta-Pitaka, "Basket of Discourses", is the source for the dhamma which was the religion of the Buddha and his early disciples. These discourses are thought to have been delivered by Gautama on various occasions. Grouped into five collections, called Nikayas, in verse and prose, the Sutta-Pitaka contains the important products of Buddhist literature. The first four of these collections are cognate and homogeneous in nature and character with little difference of doctrine. If these are the actual words of the Buddha, his methodology may be here preserved in much the same manner that Plato's dialogues preserved the method and style of Socrates.

The Dihha-Nikaya, "Collection of Long Discourses" is the first section or collection of the Sutta-Pitaka. It contains some thirty-four discourses broken down into three sections which deal with one or more doctrines, with many also discussing the training for the monkhood. Brahamajala-sutta, "Lecture on the Brahman Net", enumerates the rather large list of Brahman and ascetic occupations forbidden to Buddhists. Samannaphala-sutta, "Lecture on the Reward of Asceticism", is the second of this series and reveals the Buddha's attitude toward non-Buddhist teachers and other sect-founders. This is followed by the Ambattha-sutta which illustrates the history of caste in India and the Buddha's attitude toward it. Kuladanta-sutta, "Lecture on the Sharp Tooth (of the Brahmans)!', is of value as it demonstrates the relations of Brahmanism and Buddhism from the Buddha's viewpoint. The Tevijja-sutta, "Lecture on the Follwers of the Three Vedas", is the Buddha's contrast of the ideals of Buddhism and Brahmanism. Mahanidana-sutta, "Great Lecture on Causation", is the fundamental doctrine of Buddhism, while the Sigalovada-sutta, "Admonition of Sigala", describes quite fully the duties prescribed for the Buddhist laity.

Of the various discourses within the Digha-Nikaya, that of the Mahaparinibbana-sutta, "Great Lecture on the Complete Nibbana", is the most important. Moreover, it contains a continuous account of the Buddha's last days; is thought to be one of the oldest parts of the Tipitaka; and more closely resembles the Gospels of the New Testament than does any of the rest of the Tipitaka. [12] In contrast is that of the Mahapadana-sutta, "Great Lectures of the Miracles (of the Buddha)", which gives some idea of its comparative lateness. It also contains the dogma of the six Buddhas who were precursors of Gautama which undergird the Buddha "legends".

---

12. Ibid

Majihima Nikaya, "Collection of Medium Length Discourses", is
composed of 152 lectures and dialogues which tell of the Buddha's aus-
terities, Enlightenment and early Teachings. While so doing, it teaches
upon nearly every phase of the Buddhist belief and life. Within this
collection is found the concept that man may obtain Nibbana without
the absolute necessity of being a monk; that one may take one's own
life if this is done solely for the purpose of obtaining release into
Nibbana. It also refutes the Brahmanic claim of being the only pure
caste by asserting the purity of all four castes. It sheds light on
the life of the Buddhist monks, Brahmanic sacrifices, asceticism, relations of the Buddha toward the Jains and the social and legal conditions in the Buddha's time. This Collection at times portrays the
Buddha as being merely human while at other times he is shown as an
almost super-human miracle worker.

The third division of the Sutta-Pitaka is the Samyutta-Nikaya,
"Collection of Combined Lectures". It is divided into some fifty-
six parts according to subject matter. For instance, Sagatha-vagga
is a discourse in verse; Nidamavagga deals with the chain of causation; Khandhavagga discusses the five heresies and the aggregates;
Salayatanavagga is a discourse on the six senses; and Mahavagga is
the discussion which deals with the Eight-Fold Path. Of these fifty-six
discourses, the last is the most noteworthy since it treats the Four
Noble Truths, and contains the famous Dhamma-Chakka-Pavattana-
Sutta, "Lecture on Setting In Motion the Wheel of the Law", usually
described as the Sermon of the Deer Park in Benares. Incidently, this
sutta with its mixture of stanzas in prose and verse is of considerable
litarary value and poetic merit.

Anguttara-Nikaya, "Collection of Gradual Sayings", is a series
arranged according to increasing numbers, and has over 2,300 suttas
in eleven divisions. The eleven divisions move progressively from
a discussion of one thing, into pairs, then threes and so on. By the
time of its composure, the Buddha seems to have already been regarded as an omniscient demi-god, if not already a deity.

The last part of the Sutta-Pitakaya is the Khuddaka-Nikaya,
"Collection of Short Discourses". This is the largest volume of the
second basket and contains some fifteen books. It is considered to
have some of the most exquisite parts of the entire canon. Its fifteen
books are: (1) Khuddaka-Patha, "Shorter Texts" or "Small Pieces", is

composed of nine brief texts to be used as "prayers" or by the novice.
One is the Buddhist creed, while another gives the "ten command-
ments" required of monks. One of these is the Metta-sutta which requires that Ahimsa (compassion) be shown to all creatures; (2)Dham-
ma-nada, "The Way of Truth" or "Words of Religion", is an anthology
of maxims used to express the ethical doctrines of Buddhism, and is
the most familar and longest known work in Buddhist literature. At
least half of its 423 stanzas are found in other Pali canonical writ-
ings; Udana, "Heartfelt Sayings" or "Solemn Utterances", is composed
of old sayings in prose and verse and is a glorification of the Buddhist ideal of life and the endless bliss of Nibbana; (4) Itiyuttaka,
"Sayings of the Buddha", says the same thing twice with the first
time being prose and the second, verse; (5) Sutta-Nipata, "Collected
Discourses", contains poetical suttas of ancient and early Buddhism
which provide insight into the earlier phases of the Buddhist doctrines and legends; (6) Vimana Vatthu, "Stories of Celestial Man-
sions"; (7) Petavatthu, "Stories of Departed Spirits"; (8) Theragatha,
"Psalms of the Brethren"; (9) Therigatha, "Psalms of the Sisters"
are the songs of the monks and nuns of some literary merit. They
exalt mental calm as an ideal, and praise the values of Buddhist ethical
doctrines as experienced in personal life; (10) Jataka, "Birth Stories"
of the Buddha, which number some 550 in total; (11) Niddesa, "Expo-
sitions"; (12) Palisambhida, "Analytical Knowledge"; (13) Apadana,
"Lives of the Saints"; (14) Buddhavamsa, "The History of the Buddha";
and (15) Cariva Pitaka, "Modes of Conduct", which is written in
simple, conventional language and gives guidance concerning the
requirements for understanding and for the temperament of the
untrained laity. [13]

Abhidhamma Pitaka, "Basket of Ultimate Things" or "Basket of
Higher Religion", treats the same subjects as does the Sutta-Pitaka,
but in a philosophical, ethical, psychological and scholastic manner.
It is divided into seven divisions: (1) Dhammasangani, "Enumeration
of Phenomena"; (2) Vibhanga, "Book of Analysis"; (3) Dhitudatha,
"Treatise on the Elements"; (4) Puggalapannatti, "Book of Human Types"
(5) Kathavatthu, "Points of Controversy"; (6) Yamaka, "Book of Pairs";
and (7) Patthana, "On Relations".

In this Third Basket, the basic doctrines of Buddhism are system-
atically elucidated in the form of a catechism with questions and answers. From the standpoint of the philosophical, physiological and
psychological, this Basket is essential to a full understanding of Buddhis

13. Ibid

146

Yet, it is not nearly so popular with Western Buddhists as are the other two Baskets. Nevertheless, Buddhists seem to believe that the Tipitaka contains everything which is essential for obtaining and following the Path to Nibbana. [14] The Pali canon, as accepted by the Thai Buddhists, was formulated in India except for such additions as were added by monks in Ceylon. It is the basis for a culture quite different from that of the West.

BUDDHIST TEACHINGS

1. THE ORIGIN OF MAN IS UNKNOWN.

The earlies point is not revealed of the traveling on of beings clothed in ignorance, (Samyutta Nikaya 15:1:1). Without a cause and unknown is the life of mortals in this world (Sutta Nipata).

2. THERE IS NO ETERNAL GOD.

Now this stanza, O monks, which was sung by Sakka, the leader of the gods, was inappropriate . . . And why do I say so? Because Sakka, the leader of the gods, O monks, was not free from passion, was not free from hatred, was not free from infatuation . . . was not released from birth, old age, death, sorrow, lamentations, misery, grief, and despair (Anguttara Nika 3:37).

3. MAN IS MADE OF FIVE AGGREGATES OR KHANDAS.

Man is composed of five aggregates - body, sensation, perception, predisposition, or will, and consciousness.

And what, O monks, is the burden (a person)? Reply should be made that it is the five khandas. And what are the five? They are form (rupa); sensation (vedana); perception (sanna); predisposition or inclination (sankhara); and consciousness (vinnana), (Samyutta Nikaya 22:22:1).

4. MAN HAS NO EGO, SOUL, OR ABIDING SELF (NO ATTA).

At death the five component parts break up, while the life-force or consciousness enters another child-yet-to-be-born. However, that child is not the person who has just died, nor is it wholly another. The words "living entity" and "ego" are but expressions for the presence of the khandas. Therefore there is no living entity which can form the basis for the "I" or the "I am", so that in the absolute sense there are only name (nama) and form (rupa), (Visuddhi-magga 18:26).

He sees and fully knows, casually and truly, that no form whatsoever, past, present, or future, internal or external, gross or delicate, lowly or debonaire, far or near, is the either "mine" or "I" or "self" (Majjhima Nikaya. Mahapunnama Sutta 111:19).

14. Hastings, Vol. VIII, p. 87

5. ALL THINGS INCLUDING LIFE ARE TRANSITORY.

Everything is transitory, in a state of flux, undergoing a process (anniccang). Nothing really is, because everything is on the point of becoming something else. Everything is related to, and conditioned by, something else.

Strictly speaking, the duration of the life of a living being is exceedingly brief, lasting only while a thought lasts, Just as a chariot wheel is rolling, rolls only at one point of the wheel, and in resting rests only at one point, in exactly the same way the life of a living being lasts only for the period of one thought. As soon as the thought has ceased, the being is said to have ceased. (Visuddhi-magga 8:39).

6. MAN IS INVOLVED IN AN ENDLESS ROUND OF REBIRTHS.

(Samsara) is the endless cycle of rebirth and existence. Inconceivable is the beginning of this samsara (wheel of existence): not to be discovered in any first beginning of beings, who, obstructed by delusion and ensnared by craving, are hurrying through this round of rebirths.

Which do you think is more: the flood of tears, which weeping and wailing you have shed upon this long way of hurrying and hastening through this round of rebirths, united with the undesired, separated from the desired - this, or the waters of the four oceans? (Samyutta Nikaya 15:3)

7. THE FIRST NOBLE TRUTH: THE FACT OF SUFFERING, DUKHA.

When the question is asked, "Is life worth living?" the logical Buddhist answer is "NO". Life merely adds up to sorrow, suffering, to disease and death. Therefore, rebirth is endless, boring, hazardous, painful and undesirable.

This is the noble truth of suffering: birth is suffering, old age is suffering, sickness is suffering, death is suffering. Union with unpleasant things is suffering, separation from pleasant things is suffering, not obtaining what one wishes is suffering, in short the five aggregates (khandas) of clinging to existence is suffering (Vinaya, Mahavagga 1:6:1)

The eye, O Monks, is burning, visible things are burning . . . burning with the fire of lust, the fire of anger, the fire of ignorance, burning with the anxieties of birth, decay, death, grief, lamentation, suffering, dejection and despair (Mahavagga 1:21:2).

8. THE SECOND NOBLE TRUTH: THE ORIGIN OF SUFFERING, DESIRE (TANHA).

And this, O Monks, is the noble truth of the cause of suffering: desire (craving) which leads to rebirth, accompanied by delight and passion rejoicing at finding delight here and there, the craving for lust, the desire for existence, and the desire for non-existence (Vinaya Mahavagga 1:6:1)

9. THE CHAIN OF CAUSATION, BINDING MAN TO REBIRTH
   (TWELVE NIDANAS). (Paticca-Sammuppada)
On ignorance depends karma;
On karma depends consciousness;
On consciousness depend name and form (nama-rupa).
On name and from depend the six organs of sense;
On contact depends sensation;
On sensation depends desire;
On desire depends attachment;
On existence depends birth;
On birth depend old age and death, sorrow, lamentation, misery,
grief and despair. Thus does this entire aggregation of misery
arise (Samyutta Nikaya 22:90:16).

10. THE THIRD NOBLE TRUTH: THE CESSATION OF SUFFERING
    BY ENDING DESIRE (NIBBANA).
     And this, O monks, is the noble truth of the cessation of suffer-
ing: The complete and trackless cessation of desire, abandonment of it,
relinquishment, release and aversion (Vinaya Mahavagga 1:6:10).

11. THE FOURTH NOBLE TRUTH: THE WAY TO THE CESSATION
    OF SUFFERING IS BY THE NOBLE EIGHT-FOLD PATH (MAGGA).
Because Theravada Buddhism holds these four Noble Truths, it in
essence declares that a Way of Salvation is gained by means of Intuitive
Knowledge. This Intuitive Knowledge or Enlightenment is gained by
means of the Eight-Fold Path. Essentially this is achieved by a two-
fold personal effort: (a) to break the chain of 12 Nidanas (Chain of Causation) at the link of desire through moral discipline and detachment (upekha)
so that there is no cause for future rebirths; (b) to so train and discipline
the mind through concentrated meditation (yoga) that the mind is freed
from all earthly ties, a trance-like state is attained, with a final intuitive
flash of Insight or realization which is Enlightement leading to Nibbana.

     And this, O monks, is the noble truth of the path that leads to
the cessation of suffering; this is the noble eight-fold way: right
views, right resolve, right speech, right action, right livelihood,
right effort, right mindfulness and right concentration (Vinaya
Mahavagga 1:6:10).

12. FAITH IS NECESSARY IN ORDER TO FOLLOW THE EIGHT-
    FOLD PATH.
     Herein a monk is full of faith, he has faith in the enlightenment
of the Truth-finder, thinking, "Indeed this Lord is a perfected one
. . . ". (Majjhima Nikaya 2:95:128).

And further, O monks, when a brother does not doubt in the system of beliefs, is not uncertain regarding it, has confidence in it, and has faith in it, then his mind does incline to zeal, exertion, perseverance, and struggle (Ketokhila Sutta).

The Bhagavat said, "Faith is in this world the best property for a man . . . By faith one crosses the stream, by zeal the sea, by exertion one conquers pain, by understanding one is purified (Sutta Nipata, Uragavagga, Alavaka Sutta).

By faith thou too shall win release (Sutta Nipata 1146).

13. IGNORANCE (AVIJJA) AND DESIRE (TANHA) ARE GREAT FETTER
So, Bhikkhus, for the fool who is hindered by ignorance and tethered by craving, there arises this body (Samyutta Nikaya 2::23).

Verily, because beings, obstructed by delusion and ensnared by desire (craving) now here, now there, seek after fresh delights, therefore they come to ever fresh rebirth (Majjhima Nikaya 43).

14. MAN CAN BREAK THE CAUSATION AT THE LINKS OF IGNORANC:
AND DESIRE.
It is through not understanding and grasping the four noble truths, O monks, that we have had to run so long, to wander so long, in this weary path of rebirth, b oth you and I.
And what are these four?
The noble truth about sorrow, the noble truth about the cause of sorrow, the noble truth about the cessation of sorrow, and the noble truth that leads to the cessation of sorrow.
But when these noble truths are grasped and known, the desire for existence is rooted out, that which leads to renewed existence is destroyed, and then there is no more rebirth.
Thus spoke the Blessed One (Mahaparinibbana Sutta 2:2).

15. DESIRE IS OVERCOME BY DETACHMENT AND DISCIPLINE.
And what, O monks, is the laying down of the burden? It is the complete absence of passion, the cessation, giving up, relinquishment, forsaking, and non-adoption of desire. This, O monks, is called the laying down of the burden (Samyutta Nikaya 22:22).

Live as islands unto yourselves, brothers, as refuges unto yourselves; take none other as your refuge, live with the Dhamma as your island, with the Dhamma as your refuge, take none other as your refuge (Digha Nikaya, Cakkavatti-Sihanada Suttana 27)

150

Without covetousness, without deceit, without craving, without distraction, having gotten rid of passions and folly, being free from desire in all the world, let one wander alone like a rhinoceros.

Having left son and wife, father and mother, wealth and gain, relatives and the different objects of desire, let one wander alone like the rhinoceros (Sutta Nipata, Urage Vagga, Khaggavisana Sutta 22).

16. IGNORANCE IS OVERCOME BY MEDITATION AND CONCENTRATION.

If cultivated and developed, mindfulness by breathing is very fruitful and profitable; it perfects the four bases of mindfulness, which being perfected, perfect the seven factors of enlightenment, which, being perfected, perfect in turn deliverance by comprehension (Majjhima Nikaya, Anabana Sati Sutta 111:80).

Thus spoke the Exalted One: "Concentration, brothers, practice concentration. A brother who concentrates knows a thing as it really is. And what does he know as it really is? The arising of the body and the passing away of feeling, of perception, and activities; the arising of consciousness and the passing away thereof (Samyutta Nikaya, part 3, khanda Vagga 22:5).

17. ULTIMATE KNOWLEDGE (INSIGHT) IS ATTAINED BY TRANCE (MEDITATION, ABSORPTION, DHYANA).

Then the Tathagata reached the first trance.

Rising from the first he reached the second trance.

Rising from the second he reached the third trance.

Rising from the third he reached the fourth trance.

Rising from the fourth trance he reached the stage of the infinity of space.

Rising from the attainment of the infinity of space he reached the stage of the infinity to consciousness.

Rising from the attainment of the infinity of conscious-ness he reached the stage of nothingness.

Rising from the attainment of the stage of nothingness he reached the stage of neither perception nor nonperception.

Rising from the attainment of the stage of neither perception nor non perception he reached the stage of the cessation of perception and feeling.

The above is repeated in reverse order back to the first trance, then in the original order to the fourth trance. Passing from the fourth trance, the Tathagata straightway attained Nibbana (Mahaparinibbana Sutta 5).

18. KARMA DETERMINES THE FORM OF REBIRTH.

Karma means deeds and actions with results. Good and bad deeds cause good and bad results, especially in the next or future births. Thus karma (Kamma) comes to mean Fate in that the circumstances of one's birth and career have been determined for the present life by the deeds of a previous existence. Kamma helps to explain the good and bad fortune which is to be seen in the life around the the beholder as well as his own estate.

Thus, O Ambattha . . . with his abnormal knowledge, surpassing that of men, he sees dying and being reborn - low and noble ones, beautiful and ugly ones, happy and unhappy ones.

(He) sees how beings are being reborn according to their deeds. These beings indeed followed evil ways in bodily actions, words and thoughts; insulted the Noble Ones, held wrong Views, and according to their wrong views, they acted.

At the dissolution of their bodies, after death they have been reborn in the lower worlds, in painful states of existence, in the world of perdition, in hell.

Certain other beings, have good actions, bodily, verbal and mental, did not insult the Noble Ones, held right views, and according to their right views they acted. At the dissolution of their bodies after death, they have been reborn in a happy state of existence, in a heaven state (Dikha Nikaya, Silakkhandha Vagga, Ambattha Sutta 7).

Truly, because beings, obstructed by ignorance and ensnared by desire, now here, now there, seek ever fresh delight, therefore does there continually come to be fresh rebirth (Majjhima Nikaya 43)

And the action (kamma) that is done out of greed, anger, and delusion (Lobha, dosa, moha) that springs from them, has its source and origin there: this action ripens whenever one is reborn; and wherever this action ripens, there one experiences the fruit of this action, be it in this life or the next life, or in some future life (Anguttara Nikaya 3:33)

Thus kamma is the dynamic manifestation of being that produces proportionate results for every thought, action or inaction either immediately or in the future. The effect itself then becomes the cause of further effect so that it seems a process of unceasing transformation from one existence to another in the wheel of samsara (Wheel of Life).

19. WILLFUL ACTS RESULT IN THE GRAVEST CONSEQUENCE.

For the owners of their deeds are the heirs of their deeds. Their deeds are the womb from which they sprang. They are bound up with their deeds because their deeds are their refuge. Whatever deeds they do, good or evil, of such they will be the heirs (Anguttara Nikaya 10:205).

Then the robbers captured Moggallana and broke his bones into bits the size of rice grains . . .

The bhikkhus raised a discussion, saying, "Moggallana the Great met with a death unworthy of him . . ."

"Bhikkhus", (said the Buddha) "the death of Moggallana the Great was unsuited to his present existence, but suited to his kamma of a previous existence . . ." (In Moggallana's former existence, he pretended to be a robber and slew his father and mother in a forest).

"Bhikkhus, the fruit of this one deed of Moggallana's was torment in hell for many hundreds of thousands of years, and death by pounding in a hundred existences, as suited the nature of his crime. Moggallana's death is, therefore, suited to his kamma."

20. ONE WHO IS BORN IS DERIVED FROM, BUT IS NOT THE SAME AS, ONE WHO HAS JUST DIED.

"Bhante Nagasena," said the King, "what is it that is born into the next existence?"

"Your Majesty," said the elder, "It is name and form that is born into the next existence."

"Is this the same name and form that is born into the next existence?"

"Your Majesty, it is not the same name and form that is born into the next existence; but with this name and form. Your Majesty, one does a deed - it may be a good or it may be wicked - and by reason of this deed another name and form is born into the next existence."

"Bhante, if it is not this same name and form that is born into the next existence, is one not freed from one's evil deeds?"

"If one were not born into another existence," said the elder, "one would be freed from one's evil deeds; but your majesty, inasmuch as one is born into another existence, therefore is one not freed from one's evil deeds." (Milindapanha 46:5)

"Bhante Nagasena, does rebirth take place without anything transmigrating?"

"Yes, Your Majesty, rebirth takes place without anything transmigrating." (Milindapanha 71:16).

21. KAMMA IS TRANSMITTED TO THE ONE BORN VIA CONSCIOUSNESS (VINNANA).

Therefore Ananda . . . if no consciousness would descend into the womb would . . . name and form in the womb arise?"

"No, my Lord".

"If consciousness, after having descended into the womb, were to withdraw itself again, would name and form be conceived?"

"No, my Lord". (Mahanidana Sutta, Digha Nikaya).

On kamma depends consciousness, On consciousness depends name and form; (name and form = man)

On the cessation of kamma ceases consciousness;

On the cessation of consciousness ceases name and form.

(Samyutta Nikaya 22:90:16)

22. EXISTENCE (BHAVA, BECOMING) IS A CONTINUOUS PROCESS OF CHANGE.

Strictly speaking, the duration of the life of a living being is exceedingly brief, lasting only while a thought lasts. Just as a chariot-wheel in rolling rolls only at one point of the tire, and in resting rests only at one point, in exactly the same way the life of a living being lasts only for the period of one thought. As soon as that thought has ceased, the being is said to have ceased.

As it has been said:"The being of a past moment of thought has lived, but does not now live, nor will it live (in the future).

The being of a future moment of thought will live, but has not lived (in the past) nor does it live (now).

The being of the present moment of thought does live, but has not lived, nor will it live" (Visuddhi-Magga 8:39).

23. THERE ARE THIRTY-ONE PLANES OF EXISTENCE.

The realm of punishment, the realm of sensual bliss, the realm of form, and the realm of formlessness - are the four realms.

The realm of punishment is fourfold: hell, the animal kingdom the plane of spirits, and the plane of demons or asuras.

The realm of sensual bliss is sevenfold: the plane of human beings, the six devalokas or heavenly realms . . .

The realm of form, rupalokas is sixteenfold: being the realm of Brahma and other gods . . .

The realm of formlessness is fourfold: being infinity of space, infinity of consciousness, the plane of nothingness, and that of neither perception nor non-perception. (Abhighammattha Sanghaha 2:6:10)

24. AN ARAHAT IS ONE WHO HAS ATTAINED ENLIGHTENMENT.

Thus the elder Sona, abiding alone, secluded, vigilant, ardent and resolute, in no time, with that purpose for which noble youths duly go forth to a houseless life, in this actual life himself realized by higher knowledge the supreme end of the religious life, and having attained it, abode in it.

He realized that rebirth is destroyed, the religious life has been led, done what is to be done, there is nothing more for this existence. And the elder Sona was one of the arahats. (Anguttara 3:374)

25. BY MEDITATION AND CONCENTRATION THE MIND ATTAINS ENLIGHTENMENT.

The forty subjects for meditation are the following: Ten kasinas: earth, water, fire, air, blue, yellow, red, white, light, limited space.

Corpses in ten stages of decay: bloated, livid, festering, cut-up, gnawed, scattered, hacked and scattered, bleeding, worm-infested, and as a skeleton.

Ten recollections: The Buddha, the Dhamma, the Sangha, virtue, generosity, deities, death, the thirty-two parts of the body, breathing and peace.

Four Brahma Vihara (divine abidings): metta or living kindness; karuna or compassion; mudita or sympathetic good will; and upekha or equanimity.

Four immaterial states: infinite space; infinite consciousness, nothingness, and the state of neither perception nor non-perception.

Perception of the repulsiveness of food. Analysis of the four principle or primary elements (Visuddhi-Magga, part 2, Chapter 3:104,105).

26. ENLIGHTENMENT BRINGS AN END TO IGNORANCE AND REBIRTH.

In the same way, O Ambattha, the bhikkhu . . . applies and

bends his mind to the knowledge pertaining to extinction of all asavas (mental impurities) . . .

He knows them as they really are:"These are the asavas."

He knows as it really is:"This is the origin of asavas, this is the extinction of asavas."

He knows as it really is: "This is the path leading to the extinction of the asavas."

To him, thus realizing, thus seeing, his mind is set free from sensuous asavas, is set free from the asavas of existence, is set free from the asavas of ignorance. In him, thus set free, there arises the knowledge of his freedom, and he realizes: "Rebirth is no more; I have lived the pure life; I have done what ought to be done. I have nothing more to do for the realization of arahatship. "This is that bhikkhu's knowledge (Digha Nik ya, Silakkhandha Vagga, Ambattha Sutta 8).

27. HUMAN SPEECH AND EXPERIENCE ARE NOT ADEQUATE TO DESCRIBE NIBBANA.

"As a flame blown about by the wind goes out, O Upasiva," said the Bhagavat, "and cannot be reckoned as existing, even so a muni, delivered from name-and-form, disappears and cannot be reckoned as existing."

Upasiva: "Has he disappeared, or does he not exist any longer, or is he forever free from ills . . . ?"

Bhagavat: "For him who disappeared there is no form; that by which they say he is, exists for him no longer, when all things have been cut off." (Sutta Nipata, Upasivamanavapukkha, Parayana Vagga).

There is, O Monks, that realm where there are neither earth, nor water, nor fire nor air; where there is no realm of infinite space, no definite space; no realm of infinite consciousness, nor realm of nothingness; where there exists neither perception nor non-perception; where there is neither this world nor that world, nor both of them; where there is no sun or moon.

There, O Monks, I say, there is neither arriving, going, nor standing; there is neither disappearing nor reappearing. It is without foundation, without action, bare of any support. Just this is the end of suffering. (Udana 8:71)

28. SOME ULTIMATE QUESTIONS MUST BE LEFT UNANSWERED.

Thus, I have heard: At one time Tathagata was dwelling at Savatthi, in the Jetavana Monastery in the park of Anathapindaka. Now the elder Malunkyaputta had retired in meditation, and this thought arose in his mind - "These views have been left unexplained by the Tathagata, set aside and rejected, - that the universe is eternal, that it is not eternal; that it is finite, that it is infinite; that life is the same as the body, that life is one thing and the body is another; that a released person exists after death, that he does exist after death . . . ".

(Buddha answered): "Therefore, Malundyaputta, consider as unexplained what I have not explained, and consider as explained what I have explained." (Majjihima Nikaya 1:426)

29. BUDDHA'S MISSION WAS TO PROCLAIM THE DHAMMA.

He proclaimed the Dhamma, making it clear with his own supreme wisdom. He taught this world together with all the devatas, maras, brahmas . . . He proclaimed the Dhamma (Buddhabhithuti).

The Dhamma of the Great Teacher, that gives light like a lamp; the Dhamma that is laden with the Way, the Fruit, and Nibbana, that Dhamma transcends the world. It sheds light on the meaning of the Law. We devoutly bow to tne highest Dhamma (Ratanattayapanama Gatha).

30. THE SANGHA OR MONASTIC ORDER TRANSMITS THE DHAMMA.

Now the Blessed One addressed the venerable Ananda and said, "It may be, Ananda, that in some of you the thought may arise, 'The word of the Master is ended, we have no teacher any more'. But it is not thus, Ananda, that you should regard it. The truths and the rules of the Order which I have set forth and laid down for you all, let them, after I am gone, be the Teacher to you" (Mahaparinibbana Sutta 6:1).

31. MERITIOUS IS THE WORSHIP OF THE THREE GEMS: BUDDHA, THE DHAMMA AND THE SANGHA

We worship the Lord Buddha with these offerings,
We worship the Dhamma with these offerings,
We worship the Sangha with these offerings.

That moment, friend, in which you invited the fraternity of bhikkhus with the Buddha at its head for the next day, at that moment you acquired much merit. And the moment in which each bhikku received one lump of rice from you, that moment you acquired much merit. You gained the inheritance of heaven (Mahavagga 6: 25:5).

32. WORSHIP CONSISTS OF PAYING RESPECTS TO THE THREE GEMS.

Other refuge have I none; the Lord Buddha is my precious refuge. By reason of this true declaration may happiness come to me at all times.

Other refuge have I none: the Holy Dhamma is my precious refuge. By reason of this true declaration may happiness come to me at all times.

Other refuge have I none; the Holy Sangha is my precious refuge. By reason of this true declaration may happiness come to me at all times. (Taken from the Uposatha service).

33. THE LAST WORDS OF GOTAMA, THE BUDDHA.

Behold, O disciples, I exhort you: subject to change are all composed things. Strive with diligence (Mahaparinibbana Sutta 5).

34. THE ROLE OF BUDDHA IMAGES IN THAILAND.

Images of the Buddha seem to fulfill a role somewhere between a statue and an idol. It will be quickly noted that the Thai often say that they do not worship the Buddha image any more than Roman Catholics and others worship images of Christ, Mary or any of the "saints". Rather, it is a means of devotion, or thinking of the Teachings which it represents. Nevertheless, when a new image is cast, it is customary to have a ceremony of dedication in which the wax is removed from the eyes of the image. This allows the image to become aware of what is transpiring in its environment.

Some images are thought to be more efficacious than are others. The age of the image is one of the elements which add to its mysterious influence, its power and its sense of wisdom and awareness sometimes called "nvana". Some Buddha images are greatly valued because of the belief that they can bring luck or influence the rains, etc.

Gotama, the Buddha did not wish images made of himself so that for about four hundred years none seems to have been made. Then about the time of Christ, images of the Buddha became quite popular in Northwest India. Prior to this time, or about 80 B.C., the symbols used to represent Buddhist dogma were stone images of a deer, a chair, or a wheel. Many writers insist that the Northwest Indian Greek influence can be seen in the early stone images of the Buddha. The folds of the robes, the curly hair, the smooth faces seem to be modified Grecian features.

The Thai evidently developed an early preference for cast images rather than for those of stone. By the 13th century, bronze casting had reached a rather high degree of skill, and the number of images made is astonishing in view of the available resources. After 1400 A.D. bronze images became quite stylized and conventional, and the faces reflected less of the individual personality. Much like European religious art of this era, both orthodoxy and religious devotion were important factors in this trend. Moreover, as the image came to represent an embodiment of some doctrine, formalization seemed appropriate.

Standard postures of the Buddha came to be the accepted mode. For instance, <u>Meditation</u> has the Buddha seated with both hands in the lap, one above the other; <u>Teaching</u> has the fingers seemingly being used to enumerate the various points of the lesson; <u>Setting the Wheel of the Law in Motion</u> has the fingers of one hand forming a circle; <u>Dispelling Fear</u> or <u>Calming Turbulent People</u> is a standing posture with the palm of the hand forward; <u>Buddha Passing Into Nibbana</u> is often mis-called the "Sleeping Buddha" since the reclining position represents the physical position of the Buddha at his demise and entrance into Nibbana. <u>The Victory of Mara</u> posture is the most popular in Thailand. This posture has the Buddha using his right hand to touch the earth as he appealed to Torani, the Earth Goddess, to testify that Gotama, as Prince Vessantara in a former life, had made 700 unselfish donations and thereby merited his Buddhahood.

The golden image in the Marble Temple, Wat Benchamabopit, Bangkok, which is considered to be the most beautiful of all by the Thai, has this posture. The Emerald Buddha in the Royal Chapel at Wat Phra Keo is the palladium of the reigning Chakkri Dynasty. Composed of jasper, and of an unknown age, it was first discovered in an old stupa in Chiengrai (Northern Thailand) in the 1400s after lightning had struck the stupa and split it open. This Emerald Buddha has been moved from time to time. It has been in Lampang, Chiengmai, Vientiane and now Bangkok.

Many Thai Buddhists include in their religious concepts a belief in a nameless, cosmic, miraculous spiritual Power which can be invoked in seeking a blessing. Likewise, a belief that the spirits of the dead must be reckoned with, appeased and fed. Equally present to many are the earth spirits, the water spirits and other harmful spirits which may create disaster or even cause death. Thus, the observer may note the many spirit houses and shrines throughout Thailand. Some are well-kept and others largely neglected. Being an individual faith, each person makes his own decision![15]

---

15. The discussion of the foregoing is based upon observation and extended study and discussion within Thailand. The Great Tradition based upon the Tipitaka is colored by the Little Tradition with the two streams blending into a molding influence that affects the life of all who live in Thailand.

APPENDIX E

THE DEPARTMENT OF RELIGIOUS AFFAIRS AND THE SANGHA

This appendix of THE DEPARTMENT OF RELIGIOUS AFFAIRS AND THE SANGHA is a revised extraction of <u>The Role of Buddhism in the Contemporary Development of Thailand</u> by Robert L. MOLE for Navy Personal Response. It is included in this study of Thai values and behavior to provide an understanding of the current official status of Buddhism and its relationship to the Royal Thai Government as the official religion. The omission of the interlocking Government-Sangha roles would create distortions invalidating conclusions made without awareness of these factors.

THE DEPARTMENT OF RELIGIOUS AFFAIRS AND THE SANGHA

It was King Chulalongkorn who first established the Department of Religious Affairs (Department of Dhammakarn) on April 5, Buddhist Era 2432 (1889). This office was within the Ministry of the Dhammakarn (loosely translated as the Ministry of Education). In 1921 (14 April, Buddhist Era 2464) it became an independent Department directly responsible to the monarch. However, four years later in 1925 (15 June, 2468 B.E.) it again became part of the Ministry of Education with the exception that one of its segments (Department of Kalapana), which handled financial matters, was placed within the Ministry of Finance. But in B.E. 2476 (1933) the Department of Kalapana was renamed "Religious Treasury Section" and returned to the Department of Dhammakarn in the Ministry of Education.

Then on 20 August 1941 (B.E. 2484) the Department within the Ministry of Dhammakarn was officially named "The Department of Religious Affairs". When the Ministry of Culture was established on 12 March 1952 (B.E.2495) the Department of Religious Affairs became a part of it. Just over six years later (31 August 2501/1958) the Ministry of Culture was abolished, and the Department of Religious Affairs again was returned to the Ministry of Education. It is currently the fourth department of this Ministry. [1]

The Sangha Act of 1962 (B.E. 2505) which became effective 1 January 1963, revised the organization of the Department of Religious Affairs and of the Sangha. This reorganization is defined in the Sangha Act as recorded in the Government Gazette Volume 80, Section 98 of 4 October 1963 (B.E. 2506).

LAWS AND REGULATIONS RELATING TO THE VARIOUS RELIGIOUS COMMUNITIES:

A. Buddhist Communities:
  (1) The Sangha Act of 1962
  (2) The 1963 Ministry of Education Regulations regarding the

---

1. Information gleaned from interviews with the Department of Religious Affairs and official documents of the Department such as the Annual Report of the Department of Religious Affairs Activities for 1963

161

Construction of Buddhist Monasteries

    (3) The 1963 Ministry of Education Regulations pertaining to the Management of Prcperties of Buddhist Monasteries

    (4) The 1963 Ministry of Education Regulations pertaining to the Administration of Other Buddhist Orders

B. Muslim Communities:

    (1) The Royal Decree on Religious Patronage of the Religion of Islam, 1945

    (2) The 1946 Act for the Application of Islamic Law in the Provinces of Pattani, Narathiwat, Yala and Stoon

    (3) The 1947 Mosques Act

C. Christian Communities:

    (1) The Thailand Roman Catholic Church Legal Status Act of 1909

    (2) The 1913 Amendment to the Roman Catholic Church Legal Status Act of 1909

    (3) The 1914 Act for the Royal Grant of Land to the Roman Catholic Mission in Thailand

    (4) The 1918 Amendment to the Legal Status of the Roman Catholic Church in Thailand

    (5) The 1923 Amendment to the Legal Status of the Roman Catholic Church in Thailand

    (6) The Royal Decree pertaining to the Application of the Legal Status of the Roman Catholic Church in Thailand Act of 1909 to the Apostolic Vicariate of Nongseng in 1929

In addition to the foregoing, there are laws and regulations issued by the various governmental departments which pertain to those spheres of religious activities that come within their jurisdiction. In addition to the following four ministry regulations are those which include such matters as the Buddhist chaplaincy in the Royal Thai Army, Air Force and Navy.

A. THE MINISTRY OF EDUCATION

    1. The Department of Religious Affairs: This Department is responsible for coordination and administration of all religious activities within the Royal Thai Kingdom which do not come within the sphere of other departments, while also acting as the agency of coordination and cooperation between the State and the churches.

2. The Office of the Under-Secretary for Education: This office is responsible for the registration and legal status of all associations in Thailand including those of a religious nature.

B. THE MINISTRY OF INTERIOR

1. The Local Administration Department: This department is responsible for the registration and administration of shrines, mosques, Christian religious institutions and such places as vegetarian halls.

2. Public Welfare Department: This is the government agency which offers services and facilities to Muslims making pilgrimages to Mecca in Saudi Arabia.

C. THE MINISTRY OF PUBLIC HEALTH

One of the responsibilities of this Ministry is that its Medical Services Department operates the Bhikkhus' hospital in Bangkok while also providing health services for both bhikkhus and samaneras (novices).

D. THE MINISTRY OF JUSTICE

Insofar as the Muslim community is concerned, the functions of this ministry include: (a) enforcement of the Act relating to the Application of Islamic Laws in Pattani, Narathiwat, Yala and Stoon; and (b) being responsible for the services of Kadis, i.e. Islamic judges for disputes in matters of inheritance and matrimony among the Muslims.

Each of these Ministries have evolved a series of regulations and guidelines by which their responsibilities are fulfilled. These guidelines also act as the means by which a religious society can proceed as it seeks to obtain legal recognition and status. The administration of the laws and regulations provide sufficient information to the government so that it can act as the situation requires.

ORGANIZATION CHAIN

The Organization·Chain for the Ministry of Education and the Department of Religious Affairs is based upon the Act for Organization Improvement, B.E. 2506/1963. This Chain is as follows:

PRIME MINISTER

MINISTRY OF EDUCATION (MINISTER OF EDUCATION)
   Office of the Secretary to the Minister
   Office of the Under-Secretary of State
   Teacher Training Department
   Department of Religious Affairs
     Office of the Secretary
     Ecclesiastical Education Division
       Moral Education Section
       Ecclesiastical Assistance Section
     Ecclesiastical Property Division
     Office of Secretariat of the Sangha Supreme Council
     Religious Development Division
   Division of Physical Education
   Education Techniques Department
   Secondary Education Department
   Fine Arts Department
   Elementary and Adult Education Department
   Department of Vocational Education

In order to provide sufficient information of the exact role of the Department of Religious Affairs in Thai Buddhism, an organizational tree is included. This is followed by an extended discussion of the function of each office of the Department.

ORGANIZATION OF THE DEPARTMENT OF RELIGIOUS AFFAIRS
The Sangha Act of B.E. 2505 (1962)

DIRECTOR-GENERAL

DEPUTY DIRECTOR-GENERAL

1. OFFICE OF THE SECRETARY
   1.1. Document Control Section
   1.2. Statistics and Registration Section
   1.3. Legal Section
   1.4. Finance Section

2. ECCLESIASTICAL EDUCATION DIVISION
   2.1. Text Books and Library Section
   2.2. Research Section

2.3. Religious College Section

3.0 Moral Education Division
   3.1. Chaplain Section
   3.2. Moral Promotion and Propagation Section

4.0 Religious Patronage Division
   4.1. Ceremony Section
   4.2. Ecclesiastical Assistance Section
   4.3. Ecclesiastical Organization Section

5. ECCLESIASTICAL PROPERTY DIVISION
   5.1. Asset Registration Section
   5.2. Accounts Section
   5.3. Central Interest Section
   5.4. Regional Interest Section

6.0. OFFICE OF SANGHA SUPREME COUNCIL
   6.1. General Section
   6.2. Buddhist Council Tasks Section
   6.3. Buddhist Studies Script Section
   6.4. Education Support Section

7.0. RELIGIOUS DEVELOPMENT DIVISION
   7.1. Religious Residence Section
   7.2. Temple Repair Section
   7.3. Engineering Section
   7.4. Coordination Section

Additionally the Religious Patronage Division operates a printing house for both religious and secular books. In each province, the Province or District Education Officer is the representative of the Department of Religious Affairs when religion is involved.

The Government Gazette (Volume 80, Section 98, 4 October B.E. 2506/1963) gives the chain of organization and details of the functions of the various offices of the Department of Religious Affairs. Only by understanding these functions can one gain a valid understanding of the relationship of the Department of Religious Affairs and the Sangha.

DIRECTOR-GENERAL and DEPUTY DIRECTOR-GENERAL
The Department is under the supervision and control of the Direc-

tor-General and a Deputy Director-General. The Department considers its major responsibilities and duties, under the direction of the Director-General, to include: (1) Executing the policies of the Government; (2) Implementing the ecclesiastical policy of the Sangha Supreme Council; (3) Providing Government patronage for religions; (4) To support, coordinate and regulate religious organizations in Thailand; (5) To encourage, strengthen and propagate the right ethics, morals and will power of the Thai people; (6) To coordinate, plan and promote ethical education in harmony with the National Plan; (7) The promotion of Buddhism as the State religion; (8) To support the Bhikkhus and the Sangha through administration and education while supporting the construction and rehabilitation of wats, etc., for the benefit of the Thai people; (9) To administer and oversee the management of religious assets for welfare purposes and for the general benefit of the people; and (10) To coordinate the various religious organizations abroad and to act as the liaison between the religious organizations and the State within Thailand.

1. OFFICE OF THE SECRETARY: This office is in charge of the Department's general government service and has four sections. Because the Sangha Act and Ministry of Education Regulations give each section of the Department a number for ready reference, this descriptive review utilizes the same procedure.

1.1. The Document Control Section is responsible for all incoming and outgoing mail and for the submission of general correspondance regarding documents; for the preparation of orders and notifications; for the filing and storage of all documents not belonging to any other section or division including candidate examinations, competitions, etc; acting as secretary for conferences for chiefs or divisions and for the departmental meetings which do not belong specificly to another section of the Department.

1.2. The Statistics and Registration Section has the function of collecting and maintaining records of temples, bhikkhus residences, educational and religious activities. It is also responsible for the control, registration and storage of the records of officials, their changes of governmental grade and their decorations. Moreover it maintains files on decorations granted to government officials and other public figures who are considered to be benefactors of Buddhism. This section also keeps records of the service time of the department's employees, items of public relations and for the registration of confidential documents.

1. 3. The Legal Section acts as advisor in legal matters, rules and regulations; it also acts as advisor in the traditional role and function of the Department in the official affairs of temples. It studies and executes such legal matters as are required in the drafting of contracts and the setting of fees for the use of ecclesiastical property and temple sites. Additionally, it drafts and up-dates the rules and regulations for the improvement of the administration of the Department and the Sangha.

1. 4. The Finance Section is responsible for the annual budget of the Department and for all central government items involving funds for ecclesiastical property; the accounting of receipts, and the expending of funds, for the general management of all financial affairs with this including the depositing of current income with the Ministry of Finance and the appropriate bank accounts; liaison with the Budget office for its own essential expenses; for the writing of checks and the collecting of receipts; providing monthly finance statements to the Audit Council of Thailand; and finally, for the purchase, storage and redistribution of Departmental items, while acting as the archives for all financial documents of the Department.

2. ECCLESIASTICAL EDUCATION DIVISION: This division is responsible for the procurement and collection of both locally produced and foreign books and publications; for the writing and editing of required materials; for the research and writing of basic education books which deal with the subjects under the cognizance of the Department; for the recruitment and education of ecclesiastical personnel, officials and other moral teachers. There are three sections of this office:

2. 1. The Textbook and Library Section's function is to purchase and collect both local and foreign books, to establish and maintain an ecclesiastical library and museum; to write, edit and publish documents and magazines which promote public moral standards; perform ecclesiastical research; to list the various documents relevant to the role of the Department; to publish and distribute books written by the Department; and, to repair used books.

2. 2. The Research Section is in charge of the investigation of evidences for better basic moral educational training; the educational evaluation of moral training for adults and youth; preparing statistical reports for utilization in predictive estimates; ascer-

taining requirements and interests of the public in regards to religion
and its beliefs; formulating adult and youth religious programs; research-
ing factors of ecclesiastical progress and retardation; formulating plans
for the promotion and execution of ecclesiastical affairs and educational
promotions.

2. 3.   The Religious College Section supervises colleges of religious
education in their training of ecclesiastical officials and all others who
are teachers of morality; coordinates the educational studies of the
bhikkhus with that of foreign ecclesiastical institutions; plans curriculums
grants from the educational fund for Thai bhukkhus studying abroad, and;
provides grants for foreign monks who are studying in Thailand.

3.   The Moral Education Division is in charge of the moral promotion
which includes both youths and adults.   This division has two sections:

3. 1.   The Chaplain Section is responsible for the moral training of
university students and for the gereral public; the training of government
officials, employees and other ministry officials; it also acts as the
government agency in the performance of ecclesiastical ceremonies, and;
as the government unit that establishes and operates mobile units for the
promotion of morality throughout the country.

3. 2.   The Moral Promotion and Propagation Section provides for the
teaching of morality in schools; provides techniques of moral training
and various teaching aids, methods of discussion and solving problems;
seeks to promote morality through the use of radio, television and
printed materials; and, acts as coordinator of the other sections of the
Department and the government in the promotion of morality for all Thai
citizens.

4.   The Religious Patronage Division is responsible for the operation
of all official Royal Government ecclesiastical ceremonies; the supervision and promotion of standards for other ecclesiastical ceremonies;
for the assistance and welfare of senior bhikkhus, Buddhist priors,
monks, novices, hermits, and the saints of other cults and religions.
It is also the agency of coordination with local and foreign ecclesiastical
organizations.   To perform these roles, it has three sections:

4. 1.   The Ceremony Section takes charge of the operation of Royal
Government ceremonies and other religious ceremonies on the ministry
level.   It furnishes the robes for the monks, their titles and promotion
and the required materials for the Royal Kathin; it functions as the agency

to arrange the reservation of Royal Temples for the King. Also, it establishes patterns for the various religious ceremonies for the public's general use. For the monks, it arranges the funerals for the superior or higher ranked ones; controls the entering and leaving of the monkhood even as it secures royal titles for them; and, as the need arises, it also acts as the agency to revoke the royal titles of those dismissed. Another of its functions is that of appointing the various divinity scholars to the different areas of responsibility within the Sangha.

4. 2. The Ecclesiastical Assistance Section is responsible for the living expenses of the superior monks and the various administrative chiefs even as it is for the supervision, production and distribution of standards required for ecclesiastical administration and materials. It is charged with the administration of religious shops and organizations, while providing welfare assistance to superior monks, chief abbots, monks, novices, hermits and the saints of other faiths. It provides assistance and welfare relief for sick or distressed monks even as it is the administrative agency for the supervision of Thai Temples and bhikkhus in foreign countries. Among its other roles is that of overseeing the Chinese, Vietnemese and Burmese monks in Thailand, and, when deemed necessary, providing assistance for religious pilgrimages. This section is the general supervisor of the administration of both individual and public ecclesiastical affairs.

4. 3. The Ecclesiastical Organization Section is responsible for the registration and coordination with all ecclesiastical organizations, associations, both locally and in foreign countries; supervision and promotion of local cults and religions; providing finances to other religions for conferences, meetings and inter-religious inter-changes; promoting exhibitions among the representatives of Thai religions, and establishing associations or centers for missionaries and welfare for them as necessary.

5. The Ecclesiastical Property Division is responsible for temples and other central ecclesiastical properties while providing supervision of the division's funds. It has four sections for the execution of its tasks:

5. 1. The Asset Registration Section is responsible for surveying and issuing of estate titles, area declarations, and detail checking; making of maps for all ecclesiastical properties. It also handles the transfer of all estates and buildings while keeping records of titles, documents and registration of all the properties of the division.

5.2. The Accounts Section is responsible for financial accounts which include that of the ecclesiastical properties, daily and monthly financial ledgers, balance sheets, etc. It also has the function of the registration and supervision of the government bonds, building construction funds, annual deposits and loans as well as the interest earned on ecclesiastical property. This section is also responsible for the collectie of rents on all church properties.

5.3. The Central Interest Section is responsible for rent, rent transfer, will application, establishing rent rates, applications for the various permits and licenses required in constructing and repairing buildings; mediation of conflicts between tenants; measurement of rental properties and the making of maps to be attached to all contracts; registration of rental properties, and lastly; it is responsible for all tasks not specifically assigned to any other section.

5.4. The Regional Interest Section is a new section that was created through the Sangha Act of 1962. Its functions are to foster and supervise affairs of ecclesiastical properties throughout the seventy-one provinces of Thailand.

6. The Office of the Sangha Supreme Council: This office is responsible for the Sangha Supreme Council's administration as it applies to rules, education and coordination between the government at the top level and the Supreme Patriarch's Supreme Council. It is composed of four sections:

6.1. The General Section is responsible for performing the Supreme Patriarch's personal staff work; the Mahathera Samagom's conferences; the Mahathera Samagom's informational services of news and publications the general administration of the Supreme Patriarch and the Supreme Council, and the execution of any other administrative tasks not assigned to another section of the Secretariat.

6.2. The Buddhist Council Tasks Section is responsible for the appointment and dismissal of ranking monks, chief monks, monks who may ordain, and the selection of abbots; for the granting of permission for bhikkhus to travel abroad; obtaining permission for the acceptance of contributions for particular causes; the investigation, examination and punishment of bhikkhus and novices charged with violations of the Sangha discipline or other regulations requiring serious actions; and the registration of all monks of other religious orders in Thailand.

6.3.   The Buddhist Studies Script Section is responsible for performing tasks as assigned by the chiefs of the Pali and Dhamma preaching branches which are concerned with the yearly examinations in these subjects; supplying stationary and transportation fares, food; keeping records of graduation lists, checking registrations, and issuing letters of recomendation or documents of qualification as required by the various government offices; publishing various types of essential forms; issuing graduation certificates and certification, or replacing those which are lost or mutilated. Included among such certificates are those essential for securing military exemption. It also makes a curriculum for the study of Buddhist Scriptures and supervises the standards established for the study of this subject.

This section is also responsible for the budget that supports Buddhist scripture studies; for the promotion and abolition of such schools; for that of the Dhamma, Pali and Pali vocation education branches. It handles funds to be distributed in accord with the budget of the central ecclesiastical property; coodination with those who establish public schools on land ôwned by the wats; and the supervision and sales distribution of books written in support of the Buddhist Scriptures curriculum.

6.4.   The Education Support Section is responsible for the program planning for monks to perform, at their convenience, the public services and ceremonies; for monks to provide their services for the benefit of the public from time to time.   The participation of the Sangha members in cooperation with the government and its public charity organizations is also part of the Public Service Section.

7. The Religious Development Division is responsible for the construction, repair and abolition of monasteries. It has four sections:

7.1.   The Religious Residence Section is responsible for the construction, establishment, merger, transfer and abolition of sacred properties in compliance with the Ministry of Education's regulations. It is also in charge of the registration of temples and religious residences of other religious bodies throughout Thailand. It makes and keeps temple records of all faiths; provides care of religious buildings and other sacred places while providing supervision of the use of such places in accordance with the policies of the Sangha and the government.

7.2.   The Temple Repair Section is responsible for the development of temples (wats and monasteries) according to government policy so that these stay in good repair. It also constructs and repairs those religious buildings within the Department's responsibility; it inspects and maintains some temples because of their cultural and social value for the Thai peoples even after their religious use is discontinued.

7.3. The Engineering Section is responsible for planning wats, residences and other religious buildings. It also designs the various sacred objects and furniture for these buildings. It checks plans for temple construction and repair, estimates costs; supervises the preparation of sculptures and other fine arts for the sacred places as a part of its responsibility.

7.4. The Coordination Section is responsible for the coordination of temple development with the appropriate departments of all other Ministeries involved in the Government's projects of nation development. It also seeks public cooperation in temple building and beautification. Moreover, it inspects and supervises the work in accord with Sangha and governmental policies. This section also acts as secretary and administrator of the Board of Directors of Temple Development.

THE SANGHA

When the Thai government established itself at Ayuthia in the middle of the 14th century, the King led in the development of the Sangha which had been destroyed by the strife and warfare which allowed the Thai to become a nation. At that time, he sent a royal mission to Ceylon to secure the proper number of bhikkhus and copies of the Tipitaka.[2] Later, in 1750, as the King of Ceylon sought to rebuild his nation, it was necessary for such Thai help to be sent to him. Upon his request, the Thai king sent both monks and sacred scriptures so that the Sangha might be restored in Ceylon.[3]

The King of Thailand, as Head of both State and Buddhism, formerly supervised and regulated the Sangha himself. But it appears that royal interference with the purely internal affairs of the Sangha was comparatively rare. As the Sangha expanded, it even became quite autonomous at times. As it grew, there developed an administrative body of senior monks, called "Theras" or "Elders", which largely controlled

---

2. Bhikkhu Ananda Maitreya, "Buddhism in Theravada Countries" Kenneth W. Morgan (Editor) The Path of the Buddha, New York, The Ronald Press Company, 1956, p.121.

3. Ibid, p.121.

the Sangha. Under the Sangha Act of 1962, the legislative authority of the Sangha resides in the State. Therefore, the Government through the Department of Religious Affairs, in cooperation with the Sangha, provides those laws deemed necessary or helpful for Buddhism, and also for all other religious bodies in Thailand. The basic laws relating to the Sangha since the beginning of this century are: (1) The Administration of the Sangha Act, 1903; (2) The Sangha Act of 1941; and (3) The Sangha Act of 1962.

Under the Sangha Act of 1941, the Sangha organization was modelled after the parliamentary form of government. Separation and balance of power were designed so that each of the three major bodies of the Sangha could utilize checks and balances against each other. The three bodies of the Sangha were the Sangha Sabha, "legislature"; the Sangha Montri, "executive"; and the Vinayadhara, "judiciary". However, the discordant reaction over the mixture of politics and ecclesiastical matters over-shadowed the successes of this system. Thus, a radical reorganization of the Sangha was created by the 1962 Sangha Act which became effective 1 January 1963.

The declared purpose of the 1962 Sangha Act was to make the Sangha similar to what it was in the Buddha's lifetime. Also, this reorganization was made to support Buddhism better as the State religion-since its philosophy and culture have become so deeply ingrained in the Thai national character. [4] Undoubtedly, the "organizational structure of the Sangha or Monastic Order is one of the factors contributing to the strength of Thai Buddhism."[5] Its pyramidal structure permits the rapid dissemination of information and instructions from the highest level, the Supreme Patriarch, to monks in the most distant temples. Moreover, this well-structured hierarchial system provides the means of careful supervision and discipline for the approximately quarter of a million bhikkhus and novices.

SUPREME PATRIARCH: The top official of the Thai Sangha is the Supreme Patriarch. His title is Sakala Sanghaparinayaka Somdej Phra

---

4. Field Marshal Srisdi Dhanarajata, Prime Minister of Thailand in his 21 January 1963 address to the Mahathera Samago, the Sangha Supreme Council, Reported in the Thailand Official Yearbook 1964, Bangkok, Government House Printing Office, p. 503.

5. Kenneth W. Wells, Thai Buddhism, Its Rites and Rituals, Bangkok, The Christian Bookstore, 1960. p. 7.

Sangharaja. [6] Customarily, the Supreme Patriarch is appointed by the
King after a selection based upon consideration of rank and ability within the Sangha. Ordinarily, he occupies his office until death. [7] When
the Supreme Patriarch is of royal blood, he is referred to as Prince Patriarch. Some Patriarchs may even be raised in rank by the King in
order to merit the title more fully. [8] The Supreme Patriarch is responsible for all the ecclesiastical affairs of the Thai Buddhist Order. [9]

THE MAHATHERA SAMAGOM: The Mahathera Samagom is the
Thai Sangha Supreme Council. It is the second level of the Sangha
administration. Under the 1962 Sangha Act, the Sangha Supreme Coun-
cil is the authority for all ecclesiastical matters within the Buddhist
Order. [10] The membership of the Sangha Supreme Council consists
of Sakala Sanghaparinayaka Somdej Phra Sangharaja, the Supreme
Patriarch as President; all four of the Somdej Phra Raja Ganas (the
highest Sangha dignitaries of the hierarchy next in rank to the Supreme
Patriarch) who are ex officio members; and, four to eight Phra Raja
Ganas (Sangha officials immediately below the rank of Somdech Phra
Raja Gana) who are nominated by the Supreme Patriarch to hold office
in the Council for two-year terms. While the exact number of members
is not fixed by law, the present Mahathera Samagom has five ex officio
members and six Phra Raja Ganas.

The Director-General of the Department of Religious Affairs serves
as ex officio Secretary-General to the Mahathera Samagom while his department functions as the Council's secretariat. The office of the Secretary-General is in the Department of Religious Affairs, Wang Chan
Kasem, Outer Rajadamnern Avenue, Bangkok. The infrastructure of
the Mathera Samagom and the Department of Religious Affairs provides
opportunity for the harmonious interaction in all Buddhist matters. The
two organizations can function as members of one team when policy has
been established and decisions made. However, the primary function of
the Mahathera Samagom is that of being counsel and advisor to the Su-

------

6. Ibid, pp. 7-8; Thailand, p. 503

7. Wells, p. 8

8. Ibid, p. 8, Footnote

9. Thailand, p. 503

10. Ibid, p. 503

preme Patriarch.[11]

LOCAL ADMINISTRATION OF THE SANGHA: Below the Mahathera
Samagom which functions as the central national organization are the four
areas - Central, Northern, Eastern and Southern - into which all of Thailand has been divided for Sangha administrative purposes. The Director
of each area is a senior monk with the rank of Phra Raja Gana or higher.
The Supreme Patriarch of the Dhama Yuta sect acts as its director
throughout the whole of Thailand.

Pahk (Regions): The next administrative level below the four areas
is that of the eighteen Pahk or Regions of the whole of Thailand. Each
pahk has a senior monk with the rank of Chao Gana Pahk as its administrative director.

Changwat (Province): Within each of the regions are several provinces. Since there are seventy-one provinces in Thailand, the average
for each pahk will be about four provinces. The Sangha director of each
Changwat, province, is the Chao Gana Changwat. This is a position of
some prominence as it is the head bhikkhuship of the province.

Amphur (District): Each province is sub-divided into districts called
Amphur. The senior or head monk of a district is known as Chao Gana
Amphur.

Tambol (Precinct or Commune): The district is divided into several
tambol or precincts. Each of these tambols will have ten to twenty villages, and must have a minimum of five monasteries in it. In 1960, the
fifty thousand Thai villages were organized into some three thousand,
three hundred tambols. The head bhikkhu of the tambol has the title of
Chao Gana Tambol.

Monastery or Wat: The individual monastery or wat is under the
supervision and direction of the Chao Avasa, "Lord Abbot", who is its
senior monk. However, appointment to this office is not automatic, but
must come from the district or province levels of the Sangha. This organizational structure closely resembles the political administrative
units of the nation with the lines of authority well defined.

---

11. Robert L. Mole, Field-notes of 1965-66, On-site Research of
the Personal Response Project, U.S. Navy.

175

In 1966 there were some 24,105 Thai Buddhist monasteries in Thailand. Besides these, there were (1) 23 Chinese Mahayana; (2) 15 Vietnamese Mahayana; and (3) 18 Burmese Theravada. The 24,105 Thai monasteries are sub-divided several ways. One way is that 161 of the monasteries are Royal and the balance are Public monasteries. Public monasteries mean that individuals and communities provided the construction funds so that merit might be acquired.

Two major characteristics of Thai monasteries include the division into (a) 11,679 Visungamasima and (b) 12,426 Bhikkhus lodgings. Visungamasima are those monasteries which have a state granted rectangular portion of ground within the compound of the monastery. This particular portion of land is consecrated as the site of an Uposatha Hall by the Sangha. The balance of the site is the property of the State, but is granted to the Sangha for such uses as are deemed proper.

Normally, non-royal or public monasteries are constructed by charitable contributions from individuals or communities. When a new monastery is to be constructed, it is necessary to obtain a building permit. Such a permit may be obtained by submitting a detailed proposal, including blueprints, through the Department of Religious Affairs and to the Sangha Supreme Council. Initially, the monastery is given the status of a bhikkhus lodging only. When the monastery promoters and builders have certified that the monastery is substantially completed and that bhikkhus are residing in it for Lent, its legal status is changed to Visungamasima. [12]

The Sangha Act of 1962 states that monasteries without resident bhikkhus are to be regarded as uninhabited monasteries. They are to be transferred to the General Fund of the Sangha so that they can be maintained. This fund is the one which budgets for the general promotion of Buddhism. In spite of the belief that bhikkhus enable the laity to acquire merit, with proximity to an occupied monastery desirable, there were some 4,380 uninhabited monasteries in 1963. [13]

Theravada Buddhism in Thailand is divided into two major denominations with the Mahanikaya having 23,082 monasteries, while the Dhammayuttika has 1,023 in 1966. Dhammayuttika is the donomination started by King Mongkut when he sought closer adherence to the Dhamma

---

12. Thailand Yearbook 1964, p. 505

13. Ibid, p. 505

The ideas advocated and the practices followed cause this group to be considered the "Puritans" of Thai Buddhism by some people. The measure of influence which the Dhammayuttika has asserted cannot be easily measured since the Mahanikaya has been affected by these doctrines also.

ECCLESIASTICAL RANK: The Sangha Hierarchy may be classified in four ways: (a) by scholarship or learning, (b) by seniority, (c) by Sangha administrative position, and (d) by title. However, this classification merely presents four aspects of the same group of men.[14]

(a) Rank by Reason of Scholarship: Novices and monks are expected to continue their Pali studies until they have passed through the third and second class and have passed their examination for first class Nak Dhamma. Above these basic classes and grades of Pali scripture are the seven grades of Parien. These seven grades include the continued study of the Tipitaka and the more difficult doctrines of Buddhist philosophy in Pali and Cambodian. The seven Parien grades run from Prayoga Three up to Prayoga Nine which is the highest. Monks of the Parien class may carry elaborately decorated red and gold cloth fans as an indication of their rank. Some, when signing their names, may add P7, P8 or P9, indicating their scholarly achievement even as some people follow the parctice of listing academic degrees after their names. These students of the Pali are given the title of "Maha".[15]

(b) Rank by Reason of Seniority: In some respects all bhikkhus are on a par - all must shave their heads and eyebrows, wear saffron robes, adhere to the Vinaya rules, and depend upon food given to them. Nevertheless, length of time in the Sangha is a factor of deference. Such distinctions are to be noted in seating arrangements, in confession of offences to each other, and in title. The Navakabhumi is a monk with more than one year, but less than five in the Sangha. Between five and ten years of service in the Sangha gives the monk the title of Majjhimabhumi, while ten years and more of ordination rates the title of Thera.

Only after the bhikkhu becomes a Thera is he empowered to confer ordination on others or bear the title of Upajjahava. Only those bhikkhus

---

14. Wells, op. cit., p. 181

15. Ibid, p. 181; "Top of the Class", Bangkok World, Sunday, 7 July 1963, p. 6, Magazine; "The Saffron Campus" Bangkok World Magazine, 15 July 1962, p. 6f.

who have been appointed Upajjhaya by the Department of Religious
affairs, and provided with both a seal and certificate, have the privilege of ordaining or receiving monks into the Sangha. By this means,
the Sangha Supreme Council and the Department of Religious Affairs
can effectively control membership in the Sangha and prevent the
misuse of its privileges.

Upon entrance into the Sangha all monks receive the title of Phra
and a Pali name (chya). Many novices also receive a Pali name and
the title of Nane (samanera). While twenty is considered the minimun
age for entering the Order, men of any age may enter as novices and
remain for so long as they desire. Boys under the age of twelve may
live in the monasteries as students, but seldom are they novices
except for periods of a few days. [16]

(c) Rank by Reason of Office: This structure has been discussed
under the local administration of the Sangha. But within the Sangha
there "are over forty graduations of ecclesiastical rank indicated
by different monastic fans serving as insignia."[17] The lowest rank
bhikkhu entitled to a fan is a secretary, Phra Smuh Baidik. Discussing the Sangha rank structure, one author has written:

In descending order are the ranks of Phra Rajakhana (Phra
Raja Gana according to official Thai spelling) with sub-grades
of dharma, depa, raja and six others; the rank of Phra Kru with
twenty divisions; the rank of Phra Samuh; the rank of Phra
Parien with seven grades; and the rank of ordinary bhikkhu. [18]

Another classification of rank divides the Sangha into two
classes. The dividing rank is that of Phra Kru (Guru=teacher). Higher
grades receive a rajadinnanam, "royal name", in Pali from the King
when they are promoted above Phra Kru. This Pali name bears reference to some phase of monastic life and the Tipitaka.

The hierarchical system of the Sangha has developed within the
context of a monarchial form of government. The King confers rank
or title upon both laity and monk so that each governmental and eccle-

---

16. Wells, op. cit. pp. 181-182; Confer "The New Supreme Patriarch" Bangkok World Magazine, Sunday 7 July 1963, p. 4 forward
17. Wells, op. cit. p. 184
18. Wells, op. cit. p. 184 (Parenthetic spelling by Mole)

siastical office includes a name indicative of its position and duties,
insignia of rank and stated income. Such titles carry certain preroga-
tives, such as a specified number of subordinate staff members or
assistants.[19] These titles or ranks, bestowed by the King, are permanent unless revoked by the royal government in the name of the monarch or unless the individual is elevated through promotion and a new
name, title or rank are granted.

Symbols of rank are given at the time rank is bestowed on the
higher clergy. Such articles of rank marking are called Kruang yot.
The Phra Kru (Guru = teacher) is entitled to carry a special cloth
bag slung from the shoulder. The Phra Raja Gana receive silk cloth
and niello (precious metal inlay work) boxes as insignia of rank. The
highest rank, except for the Supreme Patriarch, has twenty-four articles which include niello utensils and cloth with symbolic designs.
The fan is normally the insignia of rank most in evidence.[20]

The 1962 statistics of the Department of Religious Affairs says
that there were 238,570 bhikkhus and Samaneras (novices) in Thailand
that year. Some 18,516 were Instructors of the Pariyatti Dhamma, i.e.
the study of Pali scriptures. 1966 figures of the Sangha divide the Thai
Bhikkhus by rank, grade and official monks as:[21]

Somdej Phra Sangharaja	1
Somdej Phra Raja Ganas	4
Phra Raja Ganas (1)	6
Phra Raja Ganas (2)	-
Phra Raja Ganas (Dhamma dignitary)	25
Phra Raja Ganas (Dev. Dignitary)	40
Phra Raja Ganas (Raj. Dignitary)	110
Phra Raja Ganas (General Dignitary)	282
Phra Gru (Dignitary)	2,301

Official Monks

Region Governor monks	21
Provincial Governor monks	109

19. Confer Wells, op. cit. p. 184
20. Mole, Field-notes; also Wells, op. cit. p. 4 (Four bhikkhus of
the highest rank are those of Somdej Phra Raja Gana rank)
21. Thailand Yearbook 1964, pp. 505-506; The Annual Report of
Religious Activities for 1966 by the Department of Religious Affairs,
Ministry of Education

District Governor monks	559
Precinct Governor monks	3,636
Abbots	24,105

ORGANIZED DISSEMINATION OF BUDDHISM: The Sangha utilizes several means in its promotion of Buddhism. These include
(a) education, (b) public education, (c) preaching the dhamma, (d)
social welfare, and (e) ordination into the Sangha.

(a) Education: The Sangha realizes the importance of religious
education and instruction for both the Sangha and laity. It has established a number of religious schools to maintain and improve standards of scholarship among bhikkhus, samaneras and laity. Such
schools provide courses of instruction on many different levels. This
procedure is in keeping with the educational policies of the government in whi ch over half of all government employees, outside of the
military, are attached to the Ministry of Education. [22]

The most important Buddhist study center in the country
(Thailand) was founded by King Chulalongkorn (Rama V) as a
training institute for Buddhist monks. It was opened as a royal
foundation on November 18, 1890 under the name of Madadhatu
Vidyalaya. In 1897 the name was changed to Mahachulalongkorn
Rajavidyalaya, as a tribute to the founder. The institution was
placed in charge of the chief abbot of the Mahadhata monastery, who thus became responsible for educating Buddhist
monks in scholarship and science.

In January 1947, the then (and since deceased) chief abbot,
Phra Bimaladharma (Thanadatta Thera) backed by the cler-
ical council of the institution, persuaded the government to
transform the study center into a Buddhist University. Since
then Mahachulalongkorn Rajavidyalaya has become the head-
quarters for higher religious and scientific studies of Buddhist monks. [23]

---

22. Thailand Statistics for 1966 Mole, Field-notes
23. Mole, Field-notes 1965-66; Ernst Benz, Buddhism or Communism, Which Holds the Future of Asia? Garden City, New York,
Doubleday and Company, 1965, p.133 (This is one of the two Buddhist
Universities in Thailand).

The university confers the academic degree of B. Bsm. which is Bachelor of Buddhism. [24]

The Department of Religious Affairs in cooperation with the Sangha provides fellowships in Buddhist studies both in Thailand and abroad. These fellowships form a two-way academic exchange. Currently, bhikkhus from Cambodia, Ceylon, Malaysia, India, Laos, Formosa, Pakistan, Vietnam, South Korea and Burma are in residence in Thailand as students, while Thai bhikkhus are studying in India, Malaysia and Ceylon. [25]

(b) Public Education: The Sangha has a historic record of substantial contributions in public education. The Ministry of Education was established by King Chulalongkorn in 1887, and one of its functions was to supervise all education in the royal kingdom of Thailand. In 1902 new governmental regulations required monks to submit regular written reports on all educational matters. When compulsory education was instituted in 1908-9, 30,000 monks in over 12,000 monasteries were the regular teachers of almost 200,000 pupils. This contrasts with the 81 educational officials and the 471 teachers for the whole nation. [26] By 1917 the ratio of pupils was 146,734 in state operated schools and 210,053 in schools located in the wats and taught by the monks. [27]

While fewer bhikkhus teach in schools at the present time, and the number of m astery schools has decreased, the vast majority of schools are still attached to the monasteries. In fact, in 1964, the schools located in the monastery compounds represented 73 per cent of the total number of schools in the whole country. [28] Moreover, since Thai monks do not take vows for life, there is a constant exchange between the corps of lay teachers and the Sangha as monks leave the Order to teach, and lay teachers enter the Sangha for varying periods of time. [29]

---

24. Benz, op. cit. p. 133
25. Thailand, p. 508
26. Benz, op. cit. p. 129
27. Ibid, p. 129
28. Benz, op. cit. pp. 128-129
29. Thailand Yearbook, p. 509; also confer Benz, p. 129

Another factor of educational activity within the Sangha is the number of bhikkhus in the city monasteries who look after youthful students from the country while they are attending schools and universities in Bangkok. The number of these students is probably several thousand at present.

(c) Social Welfare: The Sangha has long provided schools, hospitals, resting places and wells for the public. In the countryside, bhikkhus act as advisors in family problems, as relief agencies when local misfortune strikes, etc.

(d) Preaching the Dhamma: Normally, a sermon is delivered in each monastery on Wan Phra or Uposatha Day. Uposatha Day is the day on which Buddhist adherents observe the precepts and listen to the Dhamma preached by a bhikkhu. The lunar Calendar month has four Uposatha Days which are usually the 8th and either 14th or 15th day predicated upon both the waxing and waning moon. Many other sermons and lectures on the dhamma are given on special occasions, and similar discussions of Buddhist doctrines are prepared through the mass media.

(e) Ordination: Thai males may join the Sangha as bhikkhus any time after the age of twenty, and while some join the Order later in life, the majority enter it in their early twenties. Because the essence of ordination resides in the devotion and faith of the individual, the Thai Sangha has no fixed period which requires an extended stay. In actual practice, most Thai join the Order for the rainy season, which is the Buddhist Lent. Some stay three months, some for a year or more, while others devote the remainder of their lives to the monkhood. According to an official publication, it is estimated that approximately ninety-seven per cent of all Buddhist men over fifty years of age have been bhikkhus for some period of their lives. [30] As of 31 July 1963, there was a total of 151,560 bhikkhus in Thailand. This was 0.52 per cent of all the total estimated population of 28,071,961 people for all of the country. Within this number, there were some 480 Phra Faja Ganas which made them 0.31 per cent of the total number of bhikkhus in Thailand. [31]

30. Thailand Yearbook 1964, p. 509
31. Thailand Yearbook 1964, p. 512